Life, Love and Transition: Guidance for the End of Life

Suzanne O'Brien, RN

The information in this book is intended to help readers make informed decisions about end-of-life care. It should not be used as a substitute for treatment by or the advice of a professional healthcare provider or legal advisor. Although the author has endeavored to ensure that the information provided in this book is complete and accurate, she shall not be held responsible for loss or damage of any nature suffered as a result of reliance on any of this book's contents or any errors or omissions within it.

Copyright © 2012 by Suzanne O'Brien. All rights reserved.

Cover photo by Laura Rose.
Cover design by Patti Vincent.
Interior design by Tony Meisel.

ISBN: 978-1479394227

Printed in the United States of America

This book is dedicated to my mother and father, Ellen and Marty Silverstein, whose love and support have made all things possible. Thank you.

Contents

Chapter 1. Choosing Hospice Care	7
Chapter 2. Finding My Way to Hospice	17
Chapter 3. Having The Talk	28
Chapter 4. Pain Management	38
Chapter 5. Taking Care of Your Loved One	45
Chapter 6. Active Transitioning	65
Chapter 7. Caring for the Caregiver	79
Chapter 8. Life Is a School	88
Chapter 9. Learning to Love	91
Chapter 10. Transition	98
Afterword: Hospice in Africa	103
Acknowledgements	105
About the Author	106

Chapter 1. Choosing Hospice Care

A lot of my patients enter hospice care only in the last weeks or even days of their time on earth. All too often, they come to hospice only after being in and out of the hospital and enduring a lot of painful and pointless medical treatment. The one thing almost all of them say when we first meet is, "I wish I had done this sooner."

The decision to choose hospice care is never an easy one. It means accepting that there are no more treatments for the life-limiting illness. It means accepting that the end is near. Sometimes family members or patients see going into hospice care as "giving up" or "losing hope." This is so far from the truth! I tell family members that, in a way, hospice care does mean giving up. It means giving up on medical treatment that isn't helping but is causing pain and suffering for the patient and his or her loved ones. As for losing hope, also not so! Like most people, my patients hope to die peacefully at home, surrounded by their loved ones—and hospice helps fulfill that hope.

What Is Hospice Care?

When a cure for a life-limiting disease is no longer possible, hospice care provides medical, nursing, emotional, and spiritual care in a home or home-like setting. The goal is to make the most of the time that's left to the patient. We always say, hospice isn't about dying, it's about living every moment that's left.

Hospice care means palliative care—care that is oriented toward pain relief and comfort—rather than curative care. Hospice workers like me focus on meeting the physical, psychosocial, and spiritual needs of both the patient and the family members and loved ones. We aim to keep the patient at home with family and friends for as long as possible. That usually means home care, without hospitalization and unnecessary treatments, until death. Hospice doesn't mean a lack of medical treatment, though. If a patient needs to be hospitalized or wishes to continue with a treatment as part of palliative care, hospice doesn't stand in the way. In fact, we encourage it if that's what the patient wants. Some hospice patients, for instance, will continue with chemotherapy for cancer as a way to reduce symptoms, not to cure or even slow down the cancer. What hospice care doesn't do is provide treatments that attempt to cure the disease or prolong life. This helps patients avoid futile care at the end of life. It lets them die peacefully at home, not alone in a hospital attached to machines. Of course, a patient is always free to leave hospice care at any time.

On a practical basis, hospice care doesn't officially start until a doctor certifies that the patient has a life-limiting illness, meaning that he or she isn't expected to live for more than six months. Does that mean we kick you to the curb if you live for more than six months in hospice? Of course not—your doctor just recertifies you. (Very rarely, some people recover so much that they leave hospice, at least for a while.) The reality is that the average hospice stay is between two and three months.

Hospice care is a team effort. In hospice, we think of the patient and the family as one unit of care. In other words, our work focuses on the patient, but we also consider the needs of family members and caregivers to be just as important. The core team usually has a doctor, a hospice nurse like me, a social worker who helps with financial issues and paperwork, and often one or more home health-care workers and hospice volunteers. Also part of the team, if the patient or family wishes, are spiritual counselors (priests, pastors, rabbis, lay preachers, and others) along with healing touch therapists, music therapists, art therapists, and even pet therapists. When other professionals, such as respiratory therapists or nutritionists, are needed, we bring them in. We also encourage visits by friends and relatives. I'm always amazed at how a short visit with an old friend, even though it's to say goodbye, can really cheer up a patient.

Palliative Care

A primary goal of hospice care is palliative care, which means easing symptoms without attempting to cure. That means hospice nurses like me work really hard to make sure our patients get good pain management and comfort care. We also strive to make sure our patients are getting emotional and spiritual support. Unresolved emotions and spiritual distress are just as severe as physical pain.

I once had a patient, an older man, who had led, so far as I could see, a pretty good life. He had supported his family well and been active in his community. As his end approached, he was surrounded by loving family and many friends. Despite the social support, and even though we were doing a good job of controlling his physical pain, I could feel that he was in deep spiritual pain. One afternoon, while I was doing a routine check on him, I sensed he wanted to talk about something. When I was done with the checkup I just sat quietly by his bed. He then told me he thought his pain and illness were a punishment from God, but he couldn't figure out what he had done so wrong that he deserved it. I was saddened that this man, so loved by the people around him, could have such inner pain. He had reviewed his life and searched his soul and didn't find any hidden evil there. We talked a bit more, and gradually he came to see that his life had been a good one and that he had never intentionally hurt anyone. We talked about how learning to give and accept unconditional love is our main task on earth.

When I came back the next day, he seemed a lot more at peace with himself. He told me he now realized his illness was just his illness, bad luck maybe, but not a punishment. And a few days after that, he told me he was glad he had the chance to review his life and say goodbye to his family and friends. He died just a week later.

Hospice Now, Not Later

Unfortunately, many patients spend only a short time in hospice care. They go into hospice only when death is very near. That means we're in crisis mode from the start, which doesn't give the hospice team much time to bond with the patient or caregivers or to get the patient's symptoms under control.

Why the delay? Why hospice later or even never, instead of hospice now?

When you get to chapter 3, you'll learn about one of the biggest reasons people delay entering hospice or never get there at all: The patient hasn't made his or her wishes very clear before the final illness set in.

There are other reasons as well, however, that may keep even someone who has advance directives from getting hospice care sooner rather than later.

Doctors are programmed to prolong life, even if it causes pain or diminishes the quality of life for the patient. Until pretty recently, medical students and residents never got any training in end-of-life care. They often just don't know what to say when they have to tell a patient that he or she has only six months or less to live. Some doctors don't want to give up as long as they think there's some hope that treatment will help keep the patient alive. Many see the death of a patient, especially a cancer patient, as a personal failure. They believe that referring a patient to hospice is a last resort, not a choice that should be offered as soon as it's clear the patient won't benefit from further treatment. This is so wrong! Studies show that patients and family members benefit most when hospice begins sooner rather than later. Entering hospice care early on also helps the patient avoid unnecessary treatments and hospitalizations, which really improves the quality of life.

In my experience, though, a lot of doctors just don't want to be the bearer of bad news—they can't bring themselves to discuss the reality of the situation or even mention the words death, dying, or Do Not Resuscitate orders. They've been trained to treat, treat, treat, even when treatment isn't helping. They're not trained to look at the bigger picture and consider the patient's quality of life as the life-limiting disease progresses. Even worse, some doctors see hospice as a death sentence and a defeat. They think that referring a patient to hospice will make the patient give up hope and die more quickly. I hate to hear that one! Most dying patients still have a lot of hope.

Not of a cure, but they may hope to see a grandchild born, or attend a marriage or go to a graduation. Over and over, it's that sort of hope that I have seen keep patients alive.

My personal experience is backed up by a lot of scientific studies. One recent study looked at nearly 4,500 Medicare patients who died within a three-year period. Turns out that overall, the hospice patients lived a month longer than the non-hospice patients. And for patients with congestive heart failure, lung cancer, and pancreatic cancer, survival for the hospice patients was significantly longer than for the non-hospice patients.

One myth I often encounter is the idea that hospice care is only for cancer patients. It's true that cancer patients make up about 40 percent of the hospice population, but that's because cancer is a slow disease that mostly affects older people. Hospice is available for anyone with a life-limiting illness, at any age. About 11 percent of hospice patients have heart disease; another 11 percent have dementia or Alzheimer's disease. About 15 percent have general debility from old age, and about 8 percent have lung disease. Many patients with progressive illnesses, such as Parkinson's disease, multiple sclerosis, AIDS, and ALS, also find hospice is the ideal way to spend their last days.

Final Days

People approaching their final days have little time left on this earth. As this realization sinks in, I see a very wide range of responses from my patients.

Some are angry. They may feel rage against the universe for doing this to them. Sometimes the anger comes from feeling helpless or isolated and alone. For many, the anger is from the loss of control that comes near the end of a life-limiting illness. Some of my patients, I think, have always just been angry or hostile people. Because that's their usual response to any difficult situation, it's their response as they face death as well.

Other patients are just in denial. Despite their worsening symptoms, despite the drugs, despite my visits, and despite what their family says, they deny that death is near. Why do they refuse to see the obvious? Denial is an unconscious mental process that helps protect us against overwhelming reality. Patients who deny that their time here on earth is short may just need some time to cope with the reality. Some are so fearful of the future that they deny it instead. What I often find, however, is that patients are in denial because nobody—not their doctors, not their family—has actually sat down and told them, in ways they can understand, exactly what their situation is. The family sometimes gets this backward. They think because the patient is in denial, that means he or she doesn't want to know the truth. The patient may refuse to discuss it at all or may say something like, "It's in God's hands now," which could lead the family to think that he or she doesn't want to know any more. The family members themselves could also be in deep denial, for their own reasons. If they're in denial, they're sure not going to talk frankly with their dying loved one.

In my experience, most patients who are in denial haven't been truly informed about their condition. I've found that most really do want to know what's happening to them, but they don't know how to ask the simple question, "Am I dying?" Even if they do, they often can't get anyone to give them a straight answer. Because patients can usually sense that I'm very empathetic, they often ask me instead of asking a family member or doctor. I try to give as honest an answer as I can, while also being very reassuring about ongoing care and pain management. The one thing I never do is challenge someone who's in denial about death. If the person doesn't want to think about death, we have to respect that as his or her right.

Depression is a fairly common response to dying—I see it a lot, even in people who weren't the type to get depressed before they got sick. It's not surprising that dying people often feel depression symptoms such as hopelessness, despair, guilt, and inability to feel pleasure. Sometimes it can be hard to tell if the patient is genuinely depressed or has depression symptoms from medication or from being cognitively impaired by a stroke or Alzheimer's. If the depression is real, antidepressant drugs can often help. So does sympathetic listening. What doesn't help are family members coming into the room and practically ordering the patient to cheer up.

Anxiety, fear, and worry are very common emotions near the end of life. Patients fear death. They worry that they'll be abandoned, that they'll die alone, that they won't get good pain relief, that they'll be dependent, that there won't be enough money for their care, that the loved ones they leave behind won't be able to manage. They worry about all the things we all think about late at night when we can't sleep.

Sadly, some of my patients also have deep spiritual or emotional turmoil near the end of their lives. They feel guilt over past actions and failed personal relations. They may feel guilty about being so dependent on others and feel that they're a burden. Some feel despair and can't find meaning in their life anymore. Some have religious doubts or fears, which can be very distressing.

Most of my patients understand their condition. Most face their death with courage and grace. Even the calmest patients, however, can have moments of fear, despair, depression, worry, and doubt. I can often sense that a patient is feeling troubled. I don't press them to say anything, but I find that they will often tell me how they feel or what concerns them rather than say these things to their family and friends. I always listen without ever minimizing how the patient feels or trying to talk him or her out of a sad mood. Dying is hard, with a lot of emotional stress and many ups and downs both physically and psychologically. My patients are entitled to their feelings.

Some of the emotional and psychological issues I've just described can be helped with medication. Often the real reason behind a patient who is angry, anxious, fearful, or depressed is pain that isn't being well controlled. When the right dose of pain medication is given, often the patient becomes much less emotional. That's not because he's just so drugged that he's unaware—that's a myth I fight against every day. It's because untreated pain is well known to cause depression and anxiety, among other problems.

When pain is under control, anxiety, guilt, worry, fear and all the other emotions can still be there. Anti-anxiety and antidepressant drugs can sometimes be very helpful. We also have to look at all the other drugs the patient is taking. Some of them could be causing depression, anxiety, or what seem to be psychological problems. I once was caring for an older woman who was definitely depressed about her condition but then suddenly became very hostile. Her family wanted to medicate her to calm her down, but I wasn't so sure. It didn't seem right that someone who had seemed to be depressed but otherwise in reasonably good mental shape suddenly was so angry. I reviewed all her medications carefully and found that she had started taking Cymbalta for depression. A side effect of Cymbalta can be hostility. We stopped the drug and she not only stopped feeling hostile, she stopped feeling depressed.

Emotional Support to the End

Hospice care means not just medical care but also spiritual care. As a hospice nurse, I'm trained to take a patient's spiritual needs into consideration. I find that spiritual distress can be just as hard on the patient as physical pain.

For some patients, spiritual distress can be caused by doubts about their faith in God or by being alienated from their religious community. Others just feel despair and hopelessness and can't find any meaning in their life or their death. Some fear the afterlife. And sometimes their religious beliefs are at odds with those of their family and friends, which makes them feel very alone.

Spiritual care and support can be very helpful. Talking with a priest, pastor, rabbi, or other spiritual counselor can help resolve a lot of issues. Often the counselor is someone who knows the patient, but some patients don't already have a relationship with a spiritual advisor. Hospice programs provide spiritual care specialists if you want one. These counselors are specially trained to help dying patients and their families with spiritual and emotional issues. Their approach isn't specifically religious unless you ask for it. A spiritual care counselor will pray with you, for example, if you ask her to, but wouldn't suggest it unless she knew you well and knew you would get comfort from prayer.

Spiritual care specialists and social workers can also provide counseling to caregivers. Sometimes group counseling or family meetings can help resolve some of the tensions and feelings that arise from providing care and coping with the impending loss. Spiritual care doesn't end with the death of the patient. Hospice organizations offer bereavement counseling to the survivors. When I follow up with the families of my patients, they often tell me how helpful the bereavement counselor and grief support groups have been.

Other forms of therapy that can really help patients and families include art therapy and music therapy. In most hospice programs, volunteers come to the home and work with the patient and family. I love music therapy for my patients. Hearing is the last sense to fail, so even patients who aren't that responsive still enjoy hearing their favorite songs. Patients with dementia or Alzheimer's disease may not remember the names of their children any more, but they still remember and respond to the tunes they love. Amazingly, Alzheimer's and dementia patients who can no longer speak will sometimes sing along to a tune they know well.

A music therapy session can draw the whole family together. Ellen Gross, a music therapist with Family Hospice and Palliative Care in Pittsburgh, says music lifts everyone's spirits and is a great way to get people talking and reminiscing. She told me of playing on her keyboard for one patient, a woman in her nineties. The music brought back a childhood memory for the patient—she talked about taking piano lessons. That memory brought back other childhood stories. Her daughter was amazed, because her mother hardly ever spoke of her childhood. She was also grateful for the chance to hear these stories, because her mother passed away only a couple of weeks later.

Life Review

Many of my longer-term hospice patients see this final time as a chance to look back, review their lives, and pass on their reminiscences, wisdom, and wishes for family members. I always encourage my patients to tell stories about their lives and to share their memories with their family. All too often, great family stories and details of the previous generations are lost when the last person to know a great-grandfather passes away.

I like to encourage my patients to tell me stories. Some have serious regrets about past actions, but talking about them seems to make them feel more accepting of their lives. More often, patients tell me positive or funny stories about events in their lives. Because they know I'll never repeat the story if they ask me not to, patients often tell me things, both good and bad, that they've never told anyone else. Sometimes, when I think it will take a patient's mind off bad things, I ask open-ended questions like, "How did you meet your husband," or "What was your first job," or "Did you know any of your grandparents." This often sets off reminiscences and insights that patients find very enjoyable. The goal of all this life review and story-telling is to get beyond the life-limiting illness and look at the whole of a person's life. Part of hospice care is helping our patients find meaning in their lives.

Chapter 2. Finding My Way to Hospice

I grew up in a medical family. My mother was a hospital administrator; my stepfather was a surgeon who emphasized the importance of helping the sick. I was taught always that we had an obligation to people in need. Because my parents were very frank with me, I understood at an early age that death is normal—and that talking about death is normal, too. And from an early age, I understood that I would go into a helping profession because helping others was the highest goal anyone could have.

I grew up with three types of intuitive abilities: Audiovoyance (the ability to hear intuitively), clairvoyance (the ability to see intuitively), and a general intuitive ability called "knowing." Why do I have these intuitive abilities? They're just part of me, in the same way that some people have a natural talent for sports or mathematics.

My intuitive abilities and knowing always provided me a strong sense of safety. I knew, without having to think about it, that fear is a human creation and that being sick is just a temporary state. I always knew that life transcends death, but that we all die in the end. Because I was always comfortable with the ideas of illness and death, I knew as a young woman that it would eventually be my destiny to work with people at the end of their lives. I wanted to help them know that facing death is normal, and that death itself is but a transition to another level. I wanted to help them make that amazing transition with the ease and grace, and without pain or fear.

Reading Energy
The gift of reading energy is available to everyone, not just those who are fortunate to be born with a strong intuitive gift. Even so, some have a stronger ability to read energy than others. Why? I believe

this depends on the number of times an individual has experienced reincarnation here on earth. The more often someone has been reincarnated, the more ability gets carried into the next life.

I guess I must be pretty old, because from infancy I was able to see, hear, and know things that others just didn't. This ability seemed very natural to me. As I grew older, I was quite taken aback to realize that not everyone saw things the way I did.

In my twenties, I sought the expertise of Dr. Marcia Dale Lopez, an expert in the field of transpersonal counseling. This type of counseling draws on the field of transpersonal psychology, which studies the full range of human experience and behavior. Workers in this area also study the transcendent aspects of our experiences, including deep religious and spiritual experiences and unusual states of consciousness. I was deeply drawn to this approach.

Dr. Lopez taught me that our entire life experience is to learn—it's why we're put here on earth. She confirmed for me that we all have angels and guides who are with us every step of the way. According to Dr. Lopez, we are all vibrating at our own specific frequency with a unique molecular structure. Other frequencies can feel and see us, and therefore can communicate with us. Dr. Lopez taught me many important lessons about energy and life choices. My two years of working with Dr. Lopez was so helpful that I went on for further study at the University for Integrative Learning at the Association for the Integration of the Whole Person (AIWP) in Los Alamitos, California. Oprah would call this an "aha! moment." My studies gave me deep insight to the theory of transpersonal counseling. The basics come down to this:

In life, we pick our situation. The earth experience is free will.

We view our life before we enter it. There are no accidents.

Every action we take has a reaction—a consequence. There is no right or wrong.

We can see the crossroads for life lessons. Every experience is an opportunity for growth.

We must be present and live in the moment.

Our experience on earth is all with the intent of teaching us unconditional love. What does that mean? Unconditional love of others, unconditional love of all things, and unconditional love of self.

As I studied, everything became very clear to me, as if I were remembering something I already knew. In 1999, I was awarded a degree in transpersonal counseling and spiritual ministry. Soon after, I began my career as a spiritual counselor.

The Next Step

Even as I was helping people through spiritual counseling and transpersonal counseling, I knew I needed to do more. The natural next step for me, was nursing school. I wanted to combine my spiritual counseling with the practical help I could offer as a registered nurse. In 2003, I graduated from Dutchess Community College's outstanding nursing program and began the next phase and most rewarding phase of my career. While I was in nursing school, on my way to class I would often drive past a building that housed a hospice organization. I knew, from the first time I saw that word hospice on the sign, that my career would take me to that special field.

A hospice is a way of caring compassionately for dying patients, usually those whose life expectancy is six months or less. The hospice model provides medical care, pain and symptom management, and emotional and spiritual support to the dying patient and to the patient's family and loved ones. In hospice care, we don't attempt to cure—instead, we care. Some patients choose hospice care in a specialized hospice center or nursing home; others opt for home hospice care. From the moment I learned what a hospice was and the role of a nurse in hospice care, I knew this was the area for me.

After graduation, I began my nursing career as a floor nurse on medical/surgical unit at a major hospital in the Hudson Valley. People who are in the hospital today are usually very ill. On a surgical floor, some patients are near death from advanced cancer and other diseases; they are in the hospital for last-ditch attempts to give them some extra time or to relieve the worse symptoms. I had my first direct experience with death within a few days of starting my first nursing job. One morning, when I came in for my shift, the night nurse who was giving me her report on the patients I would care for that day said to me, "I want you to come look at Mary. She's dying and will probably pass sometime today." We went together to see the patient. She was lying in her bed with her mouth open. Her head was back; her eyes were open but rolled back. It was clear to me, even as a newbie nurse, that Mary's death couldn't be far away.

It was intense. Although there was nothing I could do for her, all morning I kept checking on Mary. She didn't seem to have anyone near her—no family or friends were at the hospital. When I checked her at about 10:30 that morning, I found her mouth was closed, her head was no longer rolled back, and she was looking straight ahead. I gently asked her if she was all right and if she needed anything. She said nothing. Then I asked her to blink her eyes if she was in pain. She didn't. Although she seemed unresponsive, I intuitively understood she knew I was there and that she knew she no longer needed my care. I realized that even if a person can't speak to you or look at you, he or she can still hear you, understand you, and know you are there.

I quietly left the room, knowing that when I next returned Mary would have passed. That's just what happened. It was my first experience of seeing death close-up. I was saddened by Mary's death, not because she had died but because she had died alone in a hospital. I knew there was a better way to achieve a gentle death.

From the OR to Hospice

I turned out to be pretty good at the hands-on aspects of nursing, to the point where I was recruited to train in the specialized and challenging skills of being a surgical nurse. I resisted the offer at first, because I loved working directly with patients in the hospital. Eventually, I talked myself into it, reasoning that a nurse always needs to learn new skills. Being an OR nurse was fascinating. I enjoyed the high level of responsibility, but after a couple of years I started to really miss direct patient care. In the OR, I saw the patients only while they were unconscious on the operating table or regaining consciousness in the post-op area. After that, they disappeared from my life. I never got to know them as people and I never found out what happened to them after their surgery.

At this point, my interest in hospice care reawakened very strongly. Even though I had no experience in the area, I applied for work as a hospice care nurse at a number of local institutions and agencies. I finally got an interview to be a per diem nurse through an agency that sent nurses to care for home hospice patients. The interviewer kept saying to me, "Hospice work isn't for everyone. Dealing with the dying is hard." She was looking for someone who could handle the stress of helping a dying patient with his or her physical, psychosocial, and spiritual needs, while also coping with the needs of the patient's family. I convinced the interviewer that I could do the work without losing my perspective or burning out.

The training that followed was fascinating. The holistic approach of hospice care was exactly what I believed nursing should be. The patients themselves were wonderful and inspiring. When a person is dying, it's just as important a time as when he or she is being born. Just as we do for a newborn, we need to make special preparations and provide a lot of love and care to make death a positive experience.

I worked as a per diem hospice nurse for several years. After seeing so many of my patients die of cancer, I decided I needed to know more about what these patients went through before they entered hospice care. I wanted to know more about how the medical profession treated all serious, life-ending illness. I became a full-time oncology nurse at Vassar Brothers Medical Center in Poughkeepsie, New York. My patients were usually very seriously ill. They were often recovering from surgery or a medical crisis brought on by their cancer treatment, or they were in the hospital for palliative care—treatment designed to reduce pain and other symptoms, but not to cure the underlying problem.

Learning Reiki

Many of my patients, and their family members, were concerned about pain relief through narcotics. They didn't want to feel "doped up" all the time, yet many were in such severe pain that narcotics were the only treatment. Because I was at the bedside for these patients, I intuitively felt that their pain wasn't always just physical. They felt scared, alone, isolated, and that they were no more than a numbered patient in a hospital bed. All those emotions were contributing to their high pain level.

I decided to do some research into alternative methods of pain relief. I found that at the world-famous Memorial Sloan-Kettering Cancer Center in New York City, the ancient Japanese art of reiki was used as a way to help with pain relief. Reiki is a hands-on healing modality that transmits the universal life force to the patient through a practitioner. It helps with severe pain by reducing stress and anxiety. Reiki is a Japanese technique for stress reduction and healing. It is based on the Japanese concepts of rei, meaning the higher power, and ki, meaning the life force energy. The life force energy of reiki connects all things to one another. It goes beyond centuries and across all cultures. It may be called different names in different languages, but it is always the same vibrant life force.

Reiki is the idea that people with low life force are more likely to become ill or feel stressed. And of course, someone who is sick and stressed has low life force energy. Reiki practitioners learn to use their hands to let the life force flow through them and into the person receiving the healing.

Given my intuitive abilities, reiki was something I felt I could do really well. I took an intensive course to become certified as a reiki practitioner and was able to convince the administration at Vassar Brothers to allow me to use it with patients—only those that understood it and wanted it, of course. I found reiki could be really helpful for my patients.

The existence of the reiki energy has been verified by scientific experiments. The research and my own extensive experience show that reiki promotes healing and relieves pain by guiding an unlimited supply of life energy into the patients. A reiki treatment often feels like a wonderful radiance that flows through you and surrounds you. Patients who receive reiki treatments often relax deeply in a way that is inexplicable and magical.

When I gave a reiki treatment to one of my cancer patients, she responded by starting to cry and smiling through her tears. The treatment had released a happy childhood memory of being nine years old and in a park with her father, who had passed many years before. For the moment, reiki had transported her away from her pain and the impersonal hospital setting and back to a simpler and happier time.

Being Honest about Death

During my time on the oncology floor, I realized how little illness and death are discussed in our society. We used every measure possible to keep someone alive until their last breath, even when that means doing invasive procedures that are painful and often futile. In fact, a study published in the prestigious medical journal The Lancet in 2011 showed that nearly a third of older people in the last year of their life were hospitalized for surgery, many of them during the final three months—even the final week—of their life. This isn't optimum care for dying patients. Often these interventions do nothing to reduce pain and suffering or extend life. In fact, in my experience, the patient's own wishes for less aggressive care often aren't taken into account. Doctors, families, and even patients focus on trying to fix a problem, without seeing the larger picture. Why? Because nobody can bring themselves to say or even think the word death.

My oncology patients often had very little time left. Often patients would learn only when they were hospitalized with serious symptoms that their cancer had spread to other organs, or that the chemotherapy wasn't working anymore. Sometimes they learned they had cancer only when they were so ill that they ended up in the hospital. I realized that in these sometimes desperate and always very emotional circumstances, we especially needed to talk about death and educate the patient and loved ones. All of us will experience death. The difference is how we will embrace it.

I found myself very confused as to why we would work so hard to keep a person alive by every medical means, even if the quality of life was minimal. What are we afraid of? Why is death so scary? It's the fear of the unknown. And what takes away fear of the unknown? Talking honestly and openly about what we do know.

After a few years in hospital oncology nursing, I was ready to go back to hospice care, with a deeper understanding of what my patients and their families would need.

What Is Hospice Care?

When I was working with terminal patients in the hospital, the idea of hospice care for the last part of life would sometimes be discussed—not as often or as soon as it should have been. When it did come up, I learned that there was a great deal of confusion and misinformation about what hospice care really is. Patients and family members had heard all sorts of myths about hospice, but rarely knew the truth.

The top myth about hospice care is that it means you've given up on the patient and are leaving him or her to die without any treatment beyond a morphine drip. That's so far from true that it makes me cry. Hospice doesn't mean hopeless. Hospice means you've accepted that the patient has little time left—but that time should be as comfortable and meaningful as possible. That means palliative treatment to manage symptoms such as pain, shortness of breath, loss of appetite, nausea, sleeplessness, and fatigue. It also means being surrounded by family and friends and receiving the emotional support they provide. In home hospice, it means being in familiar surroundings, including the comforting presence of beloved pets. Compare that to a noisy, unfamiliar hospital room. Which setting is a better place for someone's last days?

In fact, hospice care and palliative treatment for symptoms is so far from giving up that patients who receive this sort of compassionate care often live longer than expected. Hospice care is recommended for people who are thought to have less than six months to live. A study in The New England Journal of Medicine, published in 2010, showed that among lung cancer patients given less than six months to live, those who started palliative care early lived on average three months longer than those who got more aggressive care. The authors concluded, "Among patients with metastatic non–small-cell lung cancer, early palliative care led to significant improvements in both quality of life and mood. As compared with patients receiving standard care, patients receiving early palliative care had less aggressive care at the end of life but longer survival." What more evidence do we need for facing the realities of a poor prognosis and starting hospice care sooner rather than later?

In my time as a hospice nurse, the one thing I've heard more than anything else is "I wish we had started this sooner." Far too many patients enter hospice care only in the last week or less of their life. Had they started sooner, their quality of life in their last months could easily have been so much better! Less pain, less emotional distress, more time with family—all foregone in the name of aggressive treatment instead. A study in the Journal of Pain and Symptom Management in 2007 found that one out of every 10 families felt their dying loved ones were referred for hospice services too late. That means those patients probably weren't having their end-of-life medical, psychosocial, and emotional needs met—they were suffering needless pain and distress.

As a hospital nurse I witnessed many less-than-peaceful deaths. Sometimes the families were so distraught and caught up in their own dysfunction that the dying person was mentally and emotionally the healthiest one in the room. I realized, when I returned to hospice work, that my job as an end-of-life nurse is to help everyone—patient, family, loved ones—deal honestly with the circumstances and get on the same page. We want everyone to be truly present during this final time, with their focus on the patient and not themselves. Sadly, this is often very difficult to do. We have such a lack of education in the facts of death and dying that patients and family can't or won't realize how close death really is. This isn't helped by doctors who are overly optimistic about the patient's chances, or by doctors who hate to give up and will aggressively treat a clearly dying patient right up until the end. All too often as a hospital nurse, I watched doctors persuade reluctant patients to try just one more treatment, or to have that feeding tube put in, or to go on dialysis. The patients ended up enduring unneeded and unwanted procedures that did little or nothing to extend their lives—and that often destroyed any chance for a meaningful quality of life during their last days. The costs, of course, were huge. Today end-of-life care, much of it futile, consumes nearly a quarter of all the money spent on Medicare.

The Hospice Alternative

Hospice is a holistic approach to caring for the dying patient and his or her family. It is truly the model for compassionate care for people facing a life-limiting illness, meaning they will probably live for six months or less. Hospice provides expert medical care, effective pain management, and emotional and spiritual support tailored to the patient's needs and wishes.

For anyone with a life-limiting illness, hospice is a wonderful way to face death with dignity and as good a quality of life as possible. Hospice lets patients live their fullest life until it ends.

You have a choice about what you want as treatment for a life-limiting illness. We want patients to exercise their own free will over end-of-life decisions. The choice should be yours and yours alone. The crucial decisions about hospice, however, need to be considered before the service is actually needed.

For me as a hospice nurse, the decision to enter hospice care should be based on quality, not quantity, of life. We see too many people spending their last months or weeks enduring hopeless treatment in hospital beds, when they could be in their own homes, comfortable and at peace.

As a patient, you must ask yourself if you would rather have six months of feeling OK and having your symptoms managed to keep them to a minimum, or go for aggressive treatment that will make you feel sick, tired, and at risk of serious complications every day. Hospice will expertly manage your physical symptoms and also help you with your emotional and spiritual needs. Hospice offers holistic care, which means care for the whole person.

Death is inevitable for all of us. Even in hospice care, I have seen passings that were needlessly painful and traumatic, but I have seen far more that were peaceful, even beautiful, because hospice care was there to help.

Chapter 3. Having The Talk

According to a Gallup Poll done for the National Hospice Organization in 1996, 88 percent of all Americans want to be cared for at home if they become terminally ill. The same poll found that the greatest fear associated with the end of life is "being a burden to family and friends."

If nine out of ten people want to die at home, then why do so many people with a life-limiting illness die in a hospital? In fact, about half of all Americans die in hospitals, about 17 percent die in nursing homes, and only about 20 percent die in their own homes. As for being a burden, many advanced cancer patients get very expensive chemotherapy that doesn't help and only makes them sicker, often up until the last week of life. That's a horrible burden for the patient and the caregivers, including us nurses, who have to care for really sick people getting useless treatment.

About 40 percent of all Americans who die receive hospice care. That's good news, in the sense that the number has been rising in recent years. The bad news is that while more people are using hospice, many patients still enter hospice care only in the last week of life. Hospice care can help at any point, especially with pain management and shortness of breath. But when hospice enters the scene so late, the most we can usually do is help the patient and family manage in crisis mode. How does this match up with the desire not to be a burden in your last days?

You can die at home with dignity and without being a burden. Hospice is there to help, but the best way to make sure your last days are what you want them to be is to plan ahead. I can't emphasize this enough, but I'll try in this chapter!

Planning Ahead

Most of the people who die in hospitals and nursing homes have long-term fatal illnesses, like cancer or lung disease. Why do these people still pass on in institutions instead of in home or residential hospice care?

One really big reason is that they never made their wish to die at home clear. Maybe they never made it clear even to themselves—our denial of death can be very, very strong. They never made it clear to their health-care providers, family members, and other loved ones. And they never made it clear to the people who might have to make health decisions on their behalf. In fact, less than 30 percent of all Americans have advance care directives. Another study showed that more than 80 percent of Californians say their loved ones know what their wishes would be if they were in a persistent coma, but only half of them say they've actually talked to them about their preferences.

I can tell you from years of experience as a hospital and hospice nurse that making your wishes clear through advance directives is probably the single most important thing you can do to make sure your end-of-life care is as compassionate and comfortable as possible. When your wishes aren't clear and in writing, they may not be followed completely. Your children and other family members may disagree about your care. Your wishes could even end up being ignored.

Juliette Och, a hospice nurse with Family Hospice and Palliative Care in Pittsburgh, told me about an elderly woman in hospice care who had eight children. Her end-of-life directives weren't prepared very well, and her wishes regarding nutrition through a feeding tube were unclear. The kids split four to four on how to handle her last days and whether she should have the tube or not. The situation got so bad that they ended up in front of a judge, arguing about how aggressively to treat their dying mother. She passed away just a couple of days later, despite the feeding tube.

Do you want your family fighting over you in court when they could be supporting you at your bedside? Of course not. The best way to make sure is to make your wishes known to everyone well in advance.

What Is an Advance Directive?

I need to say right now that I'm not a lawyer, I'm not a social worker, and I'm not an elder care specialist. Also, the laws on advance directives, living wills, health-care proxies, and other parts of advance planning vary from state to state. So, I'm speaking here in general terms about advance directives, based on my hospice training and experience. You don't need a lawyer to create an advance directive, but if you have any questions, get them answered by a lawyer.

An advance directive is a legal document that lets you define your decisions about your end-of-life care ahead of time. When you do an advance directive, you're communicating your wishes to your family, your loved ones and friends, and your health-care providers. An advance directive helps avoid confusion and conflict over your future care, especially if there comes a time when you can't express your wishes yourself. I know these are tough decisions and that these things are very uncomfortable to think about. But if you avoid them now, you're just making things harder for yourself and your loved ones later on.

Your advance directive usually has two important parts: A living will and a durable power of attorney for health care. It's important to remember that you can make any changes you want to these documents at any time. You can change your wishes or name someone else as your health care proxy whenever you want.

Your Living Will

A living will is a set of instructions that define your wishes about medical care that can only sustain life, not cure the underlying disease. It goes into effect if you become terminally ill (from advanced cancer or heart disease, for instance), if you become incapacitated (from a stroke, for example), or if for any reason you can no longer communicate or make decisions for yourself (Alzheimer's disease, for example).

The most important thing about a living will is that it protects your rights as a patient. It also takes the burden for making difficult, life-or-death decisions off your family, loved ones, and doctors, because they know exactly what you would want if you could still speak for yourself.

When you make a living will, you can specify what kinds of life support are acceptable to you and what kinds aren't. Ask yourself these questions:

Do you want to have aggressive medical treatment?

Do you want to be kept alive if you are in a permanent coma?

Do you want to have dialysis (a machine removes wastes from the bloodstream because your kidneys have failed)?

Do you want to be on a breathing machine (respirator)?

Do you want to have a feeding tube for nutrition and liquids?

Do you want to withhold food and fluids?

Do you want a Do Not Resuscitate order to avoid CPR if your breathing or heartbeat stops?

Do you want pain relief and comfort care?

Answer the questions as honestly as you can—and remember, you can change your living will anytime you want.

Aggressive medical treatment isn't the same thing as withholding medical care. You could choose not to continue with chemotherapy for cancer, for example, but you would still receive pain medication, nutrition, and any other medical treatment, such as antibiotics, aimed at keeping you as comfortable as possible. And if you decide you want more aggressive care after all, you can request it.

In most states, you need a witness to your living will. This is a good opportunity to discuss your wishes with your family and friends so that they clearly understand your thinking and why you have made the decisions you have. Once your living will is signed, give copies of it to your family members, other loved ones, all your health-care providers (not just your primary care doctor), your lawyer, and anyone else you feel should have it (your pastor or spiritual advisor, for instance). Keep copies handy and give them to any new health-care providers who enter your life. Studies have shown that advance directives don't always make it into your medical records, so hand the document directly to the doctor and specifically ask him or her to put it into your chart. Remember, you can cancel or change your living will at any time.

Your Durable Power of Attorney for Health Care

A durable power of attorney for health care is a legal document that appoints someone to make health care decisions for you if you are unable to make them for yourself. The person you appoint is called your health care proxy. Durable power of attorney for health care is a lot to say, so we often use the shorter term health care proxy instead to mean both the document and the person who is appointed.

Who should be your health care proxy? Usually, it's someone you know and trust—a spouse, partner, adult child, other relative, or close friend. Being a health care proxy is a big responsibility. It's a good idea to choose someone you can rely on to understand what the doctors say about your health and ask hard questions. You want someone who will then follow your wishes and act in your best interests. Be sure the person you appoint knows about it and agrees to be appointed. You can change who you want as your health care proxy at any time.

As with a living will, you don't necessarily need a lawyer to appoint a health care proxy. The law varies from state to state, but in general, you'll need to sign your durable power of attorney for health care and have it witnessed. Once you've appointed your health care proxy, give copies to that person and to your family members, other loved ones, your lawyer, your pastor or spiritual advisor, all your health-care providers (not just your primary care doctor), and anyone else you feel should have it. Bear in mind that a durable power of attorney for health care isn't the same as a regular durable power of attorney, which usually applies just to financial matters, such as signing checks on your behalf. The same person can have both powers of attorney. If you have questions about proxies, talk to a lawyer or elder-care specialist.

Advance care directives and health care proxies are quick and easy to do. You don't need a lawyer to prepare them and there aren't any fees for doing them. You can get free advance care directive and health care proxy forms for your state by contacting your state health department or your state office on aging. Your doctor may have the forms available. The AARP website at www.aarp.org also has links to downloadable forms for each state.

Instead of a Living Will

If for some reason you don't want to do a formal written advance directive, you can simply write your wishes down as a letter to a loved one or just as a note to yourself. You could even make a video of yourself stating what you want. Just make sure the information is someplace where it can be found easily if the time comes.

Another approach is to discuss your wishes with your doctor and ask that they be put into your medical record. In most states, your doctor will give you a form to fill out for this purpose. What your doctor writes into your record is generally provides enough information to guide the people who will make decisions on your behalf. If any legal issues arise about your care, in the absence of any other advance directive, these forms are helpful for making sure your wishes are respected.

What Happens If You Don't Have an Advance Directive?

The time may come when you can't make your own decisions about your medical treatment and end-of-life care. If you have your advance directives in place, then your wishes are known and documented. The people responsible for your care, including your health-care proxy, know what you want and will make every effort to be sure your wishes are carried out.

What if you don't have a living will and health-care proxy? Or what if your living will doesn't spell out all your wishes? Then things start to get complicated. If you don't have a living will or haven't made someone your health-care proxy, the laws of your state will kick in and make those decisions for you. The law varies from state to state as to which family members get to decide on your care—usually a spouse or adult child, or some other relative if necessary. That person might not know your wishes, or might not be the best person to take on the responsibility for your care, or might not be the person you would want making the decisions. Without an advance directive, though, you might not have a choice. You or family members or loved ones could end up spending your precious last days in a legal battle to control your own health care.

Without a living will or health-care proxy, your family, loved ones, and doctors have to fall back on what's called "substituted judgment." That's just a way of saying they make their best guess about what you probably would choose if you could, based on how well they know you. Do you want people guessing about what your care should be?

Remember the Terri Schiavo case? This young woman was in a permanent vegetative state. Her husband wanted to remove her feeding tube and let her pass away, but her parents disagreed. Terri didn't have a living will, so the fight came down to what her husband recalled her saying about end-of-life wishes versus what her parents recalled about her beliefs as a Roman Catholic. That led to a huge, seven-year legal battle that made national headlines, until finally her husband's wishes on Terri's behalf won out in 2005.

What this case and many others show is that what your relatives think you would want might not be what you truly do want or what's truly best for you. In that situation, you have to just hope that the people making decisions on your behalf are making them in your best interests.

As a hospice nurse, I've seen many cases where there is no living will or health-care proxy. Often this isn't an issue, because the person making the decisions is close to the patient, has a good idea of his or her wishes, and wants to ease the suffering and make passing over as easy as possible. Sometimes, though, family members disagree about the best treatment for the patient. Because there's no living will to say what the patient wants, I often end up in the middle, trying to explain that aggressive treatment won't help and would only cause more pain and distress. It's sometimes very hard to get people to see that they have to make decisions based on what's best for the patient, not themselves. I find it very upsetting that instead of being with the patient and surrounding him or her with family love, the kids are arguing with each other behind closed doors in another room. I know the patient can hear or sense the tension and anger in the home.

Do Not Resuscitate Orders

A Do Not Resuscitate order (DNR) is a type of advance directive. A DNR states that you don't want to have cardiopulmonary resuscitation (CPR) if your heart stops beating or if you stop breathing. You can put this into your advance directive, but it's important to remember that hospital staff will always do CPR unless they have specific orders not to. To make sure your DNR request is honored, talk to your doctor. Ask for a DNR order to be put into your medical chart. If you're hospitalized, make sure the staff know you have a DNR order, because in the heat of the moment they're not going to stop to check your chart. If you're the health-care proxy, make sure the hospital staff is aware of the order. In some hospitals, patients with DNR orders are given a wristband to wear so the staff knows right away what to do

Even if you have a DNR order in your advance directive and in your medical chart, in most states emergency medical workers will still do CPR on you if necessary. That's because they don't have access to that information in an emergency situation. In most states, the law says they have to assume you would want CPR. They'll do it even when family members are right there begging them not to. That's a good reason to avoid calling 911 for a dying patient—a topic I'll go into in more depth in later chapters.

Having The Talk

OK, you now know what an advance directive is and how to appoint a health care proxy. I hope you're going to make your own advance directive as soon as possible, especially if you're 50 or older. But what about the people close to you? You might end up being responsible for end-of-life decisions for close family members—parents, grandparents, and other relatives. Do you have any idea of their wishes? Do they want no medical intervention or do they want intervention to the max? Or are they somewhere in between? Do they have advance directives? Have they appointed health-care proxies?

If your parents or other family members haven't already told you about their wishes, chances are good they haven't prepared any sort of advance directive. You could end up before a judge or hospital ethics committee with just a vague recollection that Great-Uncle Alfred once said he didn't want to be a burden on anyone. That might not be enough to get Great-Uncle Alfred out of the intensive care unit and into hospice.

You need to have The Talk with your parents and anyone else who could end up relying on you for end-of-life care. Is this awkward? Oh, yeah, it is. Nobody likes to bring up death and dying. There's even a superstitious belief that talking about these matters can make them happen. And if family relationships aren't good, bringing the matter up can release a lot of hostility and accusations of "You're hoping I die soon." That's not fun to hear.

Look at it this way: If you've managed to have the sex and drug talks with your kids, you can probably manage to have the advance directive talk with your mother. It might be awkward, but remember, she once had the sex and drugs talks with you! This couldn't be any worse. And there's just as much at stake.

Sometimes the family members of a patient will ask me for help in approaching their parent or other family member about advance directives. Here's what I tell them:

Get the rest of family lined up and in agreement before you bring up the topic. If you exclude someone from this, you might not have his or her support later on. Also, your parent is more likely to agree if all of you are saying the same thing.

Have The Talk in the morning, when the person is most likely to be sharpest and feeling best. Have it in private, just the two of you if possible.

There's no right way to bring up the subject, so use your best judgment. You could start by bringing up the health care of someone else. For example, if someone you both know had a long illness with life support at the end, you could say, "Remember what happened to Jane Doe when she went into a coma? Do you want to be on machines for months at the end of your life like she was?" Another approach is to ask for help. You can say, "Mom, if you get really sick, I want to be sure I know your wishes so you can get the care you want.

Can you help me with this?" The local news is also a good starting point. You can bring up a recent story about a family that donated the organs of a deceased loved one, for instance, and then move the conversation toward last wishes. If all else fails, bring up the topic by blaming it on someone else! You can say, "My lawyer [or doctor or spouse] is insisting that I do a living will and health-care proxy. You haven't done these yet, so let's do them together."

The first time you bring up advance directives, expect resistance. Stay calm and relaxed and let the subject drop for now. I've found that once the topic is raised, even if someone says something like, "It's in God's hands, I don't want to talk about it," often the person will bring it up herself later on. Plant the seed and try again after a few days. Be patient.

If the resistance to having The Talk continues, try pointing out what might happen if you don't talk now: "Dad, talking about your final wishes is uncomfortable, but not talking about them now could make things a lot harder for everyone later on."

Sometimes a child or spouse just isn't the right person to start the discussion—you need someone the person trusts but who's more distant and less emotionally involved. If you feel that's the case, talk to the person's doctor, spiritual advisor, close friend, or whoever else you think might be able to have The Talk more easily.

What if you disagree with the choices in the advance directive or health-care proxy? This isn't about you. It's about the person deciding his or her own future.

Chapter 4. Pain Management

Pain relief is a basic principle of hospice care. All hospice workers feel very strongly that no patient should ever suffer from pain. Pain management is probably the single most valuable thing I do as a hospice nurse.

Nearly all people with a life-limiting disease will have some pain. For some, the pain will be severe. Even moderate pain is enough to really affect the quality of life for the patient. The most important thing to remember about pain management for someone with a life-limiting illness is that it can and should be done. We can control pain completely for almost every patient. There's nothing about pain that is inevitable or should be tolerated.

Pain Drugs

Today we have a lot of really effective drugs for treating pain. When deciding which drugs to use, we start by asking the patient to assess the pain on a scale of 0 to 10, where 0 is no pain at all and 10 is the worst pain you've ever felt.

For mild pain (pain score of 1 to 3), we start with nonprescription drugs such as aspirin, ibuprofen (Advil), and acetaminophen (Tylenol) to see if they help. Sometimes they do; sometimes they're not enough.

For moderate pain (pain score of 4 to 6), we use low-dose opiates combined with ibuprofen or acetaminophen. These drugs usually contain codeine, hydrocodone, or oxycodone. Brand names include Vicodin and Lortab.

For severe pain (7 to 10 on the pain scale), we use stronger opiates such as morphine, hydromorphone (Dilaudid), oxycodone (Oxycontin), and fentanyl.

Opioid Drugs

Opioids, also called opiates or narcotics, are morphine or drugs that work in ways similar to morphine. There are a lot of really bad misconceptions about these drugs. The most common one is that they are addicting. OK, people do misuse drugs like morphine and oxycodone, and when they do, they can become physically and psychologically addicted. But people who need these powerful drugs for pain relief DO NOT become addicted to them. They don't even become psychologically dependent on them. What they do become is pain-free from drugs that are safe and effective when used properly. Every expert on the subject agrees that dying people should get all the pain relief they need without worrying about possible long-term issues of drug dependence.

Sometimes I have patients who are in pain but don't want to take opioids yet. They think that these drugs need to be saved for when the pain gets worse. Not so! One of the best things about morphine is that there's no upper limit on the dose. We can increase the dose in steps until we come up with the amount that gets the patient to the point of being pain-free but alert. Often, once we find that dose level, the patient can stay with it for weeks or even longer. In fact, he or she may be able to cut back on the dose. Of course, pain from a life-limiting illness often worsens as time goes on. We're always on the lookout for changes in pain that mean a change in medication is needed.

Morphine and other opiates do have some side effects. Patients often worry that pain meds will make them dopey or very sedated. You may feel drowsy at first after starting on an opiate, but between adjusting the dose and your body getting used to the drug, you should be feeling alert and awake within a few days. The other major side effect of opiate drugs is constipation. When we start you on morphine, we also start you on stool softeners and a mild laxative to prevent constipation. In most cases, that keeps the problem from happening. If you do get constipated, we can easily treat the problem and then adjust the amount of stool softener and laxative to keep it from coming back. Constipation can be very distressing, to the point where some patients will want to skip their pain meds. Please don't be too embarrassed to discuss your bowel movements with me! I need to know so that I can keep you as comfortable as possible.

Staying Ahead of the Pain

It's much easier to prevent pain than it is to relieve it. That's why we start pain meds as soon as the patient feels discomfort. It's also why we try hard to stay ahead of the pain, increasing the dose quickly if it needs to be or adding another drug. To stay ahead of the pain, it's important to give the drugs as prescribed. If you're supposed to give the drug every six hours, stick to the schedule. Don't wait for the pain to start again before you give the next dose. On the other hand, if the dose wears off too quickly, it's OK to give the next dose sooner. If that happens, though, it usually means the patient's condition has changed. Don't increase the dose on your own. Call your hospice nurse so we can work together to increase the dose and/or change the medications.

Caregivers need to believe it when their loved one says she's in pain. Only the person in pain knows how it feels and whether she's getting enough pain relief. If you feel the pain isn't being controlled well enough, tell your hospice nurse immediately so I can arrange for a change of dose or an additional med. Unfortunately, the paperwork for controlled substances means that I can't always get you a new prescription as quickly as I would like. If there's a pain problem, call no matter what time it is so we can get things in motion as quickly as possible.

When else should you call your nurse for pain? If there's a new or different pain, even if it's not severe; if the increased pain med and/or new med aren't helping; if there's a sudden change in the patient's activity level; if the patient is having bad side effects from the drugs, such as nausea.

Sometimes patients can no longer tell you where it hurts or how bad it is. You have to look for nonverbal cues, such as tears, tightly closed eyes, grimacing, groaning, and clenched fists. Look for changes in behavior and activity level. If the patient had pain before he or she became unresponsive, it's still there and you need to continue or even increase the pain meds.

We also use morphine to help with shortness of breath or difficulty breathing. It's almost miraculous to see how quickly it helps. Because shortness of breath is common when a patient is nearing the end, some people think that morphine causes death quicker. I hear this all the time and it is so not true! (I'll talk more about treating shortness of breath in chapters 5 and 6.)

Breakthrough Pain

Even when we have the basic pain issues under control, some patients can still have flare-ups of additional pain. This is called breakthrough pain. Sometimes it's caused by doing something, like moving from the bed to a chair. Sometimes it happens when the patient is getting toward the end of the last dose of pain medication. And sometimes it just happens. Fentanyl patches work really well for breakthrough pain.

If your loved one starts having breakthrough pain, call your hospice nurse at once. She'll help you figure out the right dose of whatever opiate drug you have on hand to deal with the pain. She'll also get started on a prescription for fentanyl or possibly another drug. If breakthrough pain is happening more than a few times in 24 hours, the overall morphine dose may need to be increased. Don't do this on your own—call your nurse.

Nerve Pain

Some patients have neuropathy, or nerve pain. It's usually caused by complications of diabetes or as a side effect from chemotherapy for cancer. No matter what the cause, it can be very painful. Neuropathy can be treated with opioids, but often your doctor will want to try using steroid drugs first. Anticonvulsant drugs such as gabapentin (Neurontin) and phenytoin turn out to be helpful for neuropathy pain and are often the first choice for treatment. These drugs can have side effects such as sedation, dizziness, and nausea. Give them as directed. It may take a few days for the benefits to kick in. If they don't help or the side effects are too annoying, your nurse can discuss the situation with the doctor and possibly switch you over to morphine.

Practical Caregiving: Treating Pain

In addition to using pain drugs, you can take some practical steps that will help your loved one feel less discomfort. Relaxation techniques, meditation, and prayer can be very helpful. So is healing touch, but only if the patient doesn't have skin problems. Distraction also helps—listening to music, reading, talking to a visitor, watching TV, for example. Sometimes a heating pad set on low or a warm washcloth can help relax tense muscles, but be very careful with these. At this point in the progression of the life-limiting illness, the patient's skin is probably very sensitive to damage. Aromatherapy seems to help some people. The scent of lavender is very calming. Some patients find scents more annoying than relaxing, however, and they may cause breathing problems. Ask the patient before trying aromatherapy, and stop if it's bothering the patient.

Practical Caregiving: Giving Pain Drugs

For patients who are still able to swallow easily, we usually give morphine in pill form. The tablets come in two forms: rapid release and extended release. Rapid release tablets start working quickly but only last for about four hours. For patients who are having trouble swallowing pills, the rapid release tablets can be crushed and put into ice cream, applesauce, pudding, or anything soft that the patient can swallow safely. The extended release (ER or XR) tablets or capsules are usually take once every 12 hours. Don't crush these! The pills are meant to dissolve slowly and steadily in the digestive tract to deliver an even dose over time. If you crush them, you'll be giving the patient a really big dose at once, which is very dangerous.

When swallowing safely becomes a problem, we switch to liquid morphine, also called morphine solution. Liquid morphine is very easy to give. It's concentrated, so a small amount delivers a large dose. It also works fast, usually within 15 minutes. Liquid morphine only lasts for four hours. It has a very bitter taste. We're now using liquid morphine because the patient is having trouble swallowing, so don't mix it with anything. Instead, give the patient a few sips of water or some ice chips afterward to clear out the taste.

To give liquid morphine, use the dropper or dosing spoon that comes with it. This stuff is very concentrated, so be as accurate as you can with the dose. When you first start using the liquid, your hospice nurse will show you what to do to get the right dose.

We can also use morphine and some other drugs in the form of sublingual tablets. These pills are placed under the tongue or in the cheek, where they dissolve and are absorbed into the bloodstream.

If the patient can't swallow at all anymore and needs a long-acting painkiller, we sometimes use morphine in a suppository. Suppositories are inserted into the rectum. If this is the form that's best for the patient, your hospice nurse will show you how to use it.

A wonderful way to get pain relief is through skin patches that release the drug steadily into the system. The patches last for three days. Skin patches are great because you don't have to remember to take the pills or keep track of them. They're also great if the patient is having trouble swallowing or keeping things down. They're not always right for the patient, though, so we can't give them to everybody. We usually use skin patches that contain the powerful opiod painkiller fentanyl.

Keeping track of pain medication (and other meds) is important to make sure you're giving the right dose at the right time. Keep a small notebook and pen handy and make a note each time you give the drugs. Write down the name of the drug, the dose, and the time. If you're using liquid morphine, set a timer or alarm clock for four hours so you can give it on schedule. This is important for staying ahead of the pain.

Pain drugs have a high street value. They're also dangerous and possibly even fatal to kids and pets who get into them by accident. Keep all drug containers, but especially pain and anti-anxiety drugs, in a safe place.

Anti-anxiety Drugs

Patients in hospice care often feel very anxious as they approach the end of their time on earth. They may be fearful, worried, confused, and tense. Often they have trouble sleeping and concentrating and can't really relax. They might be worried about their illness, their future, family relationships, and money issues. Many have deep spiritual concerns. And all too often, untreated or undertreated pain turns out be part of the problem.

So, step one is finding out if the patient is in pain and getting the appropriate medications in place. Talking about the issues with the patient, and getting them some spiritual counseling if they want it, can help relieve anxiety. So does quiet music, a calm setting, and healing touch such as massage (if the patient's skin isn't breaking down from bedsores) or reiki. Anti-anxiety medications are also extremely helpful. The two drugs we use most often are lorazepam (Ativan) and diazepam (Valium). They don't interfere with pain meds. They're also available in liquid form, which is helpful when the patient has trouble swallowing. If you notice signs of anxiety in your loved one and feel that other steps aren't helping much, talk to your hospice nurse about anti-anxiety drugs.

Drugs can also be very helpful for the agitation and extreme restlessness that can come when the end is very near—at that point death is usually no more than a couple of days away. Patients who are very agitated or restless can easily hurt themselves or even fall out of bed. Call your hospice nurse as soon as you notice signs of agitation or restlessness, such as pulling at the sheets and blankets, trying to get out of bed, sleeplessness, and constant moving around or fidgeting. You can help calm the patient by being calm and reassuring yourself. Soft music, loving touch, and limiting the number of people in the room can also help. At this point it's important to have someone stay with the patient as much as possible to keep him or her safe. Anti-anxiety medication can also be very helpful for keeping the patient comfortable and safe. Sometimes we need to try other, more powerful drugs for extreme agitation. The sooner we get agitation and restlessness under control, the safer and more comfortable the patient will be.

Chapter 5. Taking Care of Your Loved One

When someone decides to enter home hospice care, there's usually a sudden flurry of activity. A social worker visits to help organize the home for the patient and coordinate the medical care with the Medicare or insurance coverage. A medical supply company delivers a hospital bed, table tray, and other items. If the patient needs oxygen, a different company may deliver the equipment and send a respiratory therapist to show you how to use it. A hospice nurse comes by to plan the medical care and teach the family members how to care for the loved one. Family members and friends may come by to welcome the patient home from the hospital.

And after all the activity stops and all the visitors leave, often just one family caretaker is left alone with a dying patient who needs a lot of care.

Now what?

In my experience, the first few days of home hospice can be very, very challenging for the patient and the caregivers. I've seen caregivers who were literally afraid to touch the patient, and others who ended up accidentally harming the patient even though they were trying to help. And I've also seen patients who were so polite that they wouldn't express their own needs even though they were dying.

I can't blame people for not knowing how to help a hospice patient with his or her needs. How is the ordinary person supposed to know the best way to move a bedridden patient, for example? As a hospice nurse, I parachute in, give you some instructions about giving meds and basic care, and leave behind a pile of brochures and handouts and the phone number to reach a nurse 24/7 for advice. Then I stop by every week to see how things are going. You might have a home health aide who comes in for an hour or two five days a week, and you might get home visits from a physical therapist and some other services, but basically, caregivers are on their own.

In this chapter I'm going to give you a lot of practical tips on how to care for a hospice patient. My advice is based on years of bedside experience with patients and their caregivers. My goal is always to make the hospice experience as valuable as possible—I want the patient's remaining time here on earth to be comfortable and meaningful. I also want the family to make the most of the hospice experience and not be exhausted and overwhelmed by their caretaking.

How to Be a Hospice Patient

By the time I meet many of my home hospice patients, they are unfortunately so close to death that we don't have much time to discuss their own needs and desires. In fact, many of them can't really talk much at all. I often have to guess in these situations, based on my strong intuitive senses and on my bedside experience.

For patients who go into hospice care sooner or who can still express themselves clearly, the most important thing they can do is speak up. I've seen hospice care patients suffer with pain because they didn't want to bother a tired caregiver about bringing their meds. I've watched hospice care patients try to eat food that caregivers have lovingly prepared but that they can't get down. I've watched hospice patients sit through over-long visits from well-meaning guests because they were too polite to say no.

Now is the time to be open. If you're in pain or discomfort of any sort, please say so. If you're feeling too tired or down to see a visitor, say so. If you're not hungry, you don't have to eat. If you're worried about how much your care is costing, say so. And if you feel depressed or troubled spiritually or emotionally, please say so. I may sense it, but I need you to bring it up. I can often help with comfort and fatigue issues, and after years of experience I can be very reassuring about the costs of your care. Remember that hospice care deals with the whole person. We want you to be at peace. For the areas where I can't help, we have the resources to get you spiritual and psychological care as well as physical care.

Hospice Helpers

When you go into hospice care, suddenly all sorts of people are in your house. There's me, your friendly hospice nurse, making arrangement for your medical equipment, like a hospital bed and oxygen. I'm also stopping by at least once a week and usually more often, and talking to you and your caregivers on the phone when you need me. There's also the nurse on duty when I'm not around. Then there's the hospice service medical director, who is now working on your treatment, usually along with your regular doctor. Your social worker or case worker is coordinating all your Medicare and insurance and making sure you're covered somehow. Someone, usually me as your nurse case manager, also makes arrangements for you to have a home health aide come by for an hour or two most days. Your social worker or nurse case manager can also make arrangements for you to have visits from a music therapist, art therapist, spiritual care specialist, and even a pet therapist. Plus, you might be getting medical visits from a respiratory therapist, a physical therapist, maybe an occupational therapist to teach you how to use assistive devices, and possibly a speech therapist, especially if you are having swallowing problems. And of course, family members and friends all want to visit you and help however they can.

Let's look at what each person does and why—or possibly why not—you need their help.

Social Workers

Social workers or case workers for hospice are trained professionals who are very good at getting a home hospice situation set up quickly and smoothly and then coordinating your care going forward. They're the first step in making hospice happen. They're experts in assessing the home for issues like safety problems and family issues that could impact the patient's care. Fortunately, social workers are also experts in the financial end of hospice. They know to the penny what benefits are paid for by Medicare and Medicaid. If you have private insurance or a long-term care plan, they know how to manage them, too. And if finances are a problem, they can almost always find other ways to get you the care you need.

Hospice Nurses

OK, I'm biased, but we hospice nurses play the central role in making home hospice possible. As case managers, we help get the patient set up at home with whatever is needed. We can make a hospital bed, a bed tray, a commode, and a lot of other medical supplies appear almost like magic. We make arrangements for home health aides and whatever therapists may be needed. We spend a lot of time teaching you about patient care. We also educate you about what to expect over time as the loved one nears the end. Most important, we're there to provide support and answer questions. We stop by often, at least once a week when the patient is stable and more often if the patient needs us for symptom management. Sometimes I could be there every day, making sure the patient and the family are OK. And we're only ever a phone call away, 24/7. If I'm not personally available for one of my patients, a call nurse who knows all about the case is on duty.

Home Health Aides (CNAs)

Most home hospice patients qualify for help from a home health aide, also called a certified nursing assistant (CNA). CNAs are trained and qualified in basic patient care skills; they have to be, or Medicare won't pay for their services. Your CNA will probably be there for just an hour or two every weekday, and possibly not on weekends. Make the most of this time by asking her (most CNAs are women) to help with getting the patient ready for the day. The CNA can change the bedding and help the patient bathe and dress, move from the bed to a chair, use the bathroom, and eat. If there's time left after all this, it's perfectly OK to ask the CNA to help with other things, like tidying the patient's room or running an errand. CNAs aren't allowed to give meds or do wound care such as changing dressings. What's great about CNAs is that most are very experienced. They'll often pick up on a problem, such as the beginnings of a bedsore or an infection, sooner than a family member would. That lets me get on the problem quickly.

When your CNA first arrives, I'll be there to introduce her to the patient and the caregivers and teach her about the special aspects of the case. I'll supervise her for as long as she's working with you. In most cases, the cost of your home health aide is paid by Medicare, Medicaid, or your private insurance. It's also possible to hire a home health aide and pay for the help yourself. Most home health aides work through local agencies. Your social worker or hospice nurse can put you in touch with a reliable agency.

When I tell you that the CNAs I have worked with have always been hard-working, devoted, honest people, I mean it. They can be far more valuable to the patient and caregivers than anything I do. I often see CNAs form a real bond with the patient and have great rapport with the family. Sometimes, though, a particular CNA isn't a good fit with the patient. If that happens, don't hesitate to tell your hospice nurse at once and ask for someone else. When Steve Jobs of Apple fame was dying of pancreatic cancer, he needed (and could afford) round-the-clock nurses. He went through 67 of them to find the three that were with him to the end. Your local hospice probably can't be that accommodating, but if anyone you encounter in hospice care—even me, your hospice nurse—isn't a good fit for the patient or the caregivers, speak up.

Other Hospice Helpers

Who are all those other hospice helpers? They're people, often volunteers, who are there to help make the hospice experience more comfortable and more meaningful. They're music therapists, art therapists, pet therapists, and spiritual care specialists. They will visit you only if you ask for them. Some patients and families find great comfort and enjoyment in these visits; others find them disruptive. It's entirely up to you. I generally encourage patients who are feeling well enough to take advantage of these volunteers. They provide a welcome break in the day. They can also be very helpful for letting patients express themselves. Lisa Elliger, a colleague who is an expressive art therapist at Family Hospice and Palliative Care in Pittsburgh, says, "Creativity engages the heart and allows the mind to achieve clarity." Her experiences with dying patients show the value of what she does. Lisa brings art supplies with her when she visits patients and lets them choose what they would like to do. One older woman, while piecing together a fabric collage, kept saying, "What comes next?" Lisa knew she was really asking what would happen to her as she transitioned toward death, and what would happen after death. Lisa feels that just being able to ask the question aloud gave the patient a great deal of comfort and perhaps some clarity. Art therapy is a great tool for helping patients engage and communicate. One of Lisa's patients never said much to her. One day, after the patient had been painting silently for more than an hour, she said, out of the blue, "The boss isn't ready for me yet." She worked out for herself, while she was engaged in her art, that the time when the boss wanted her would be coming, but not yet. After that, she was able to let go some of her anxiety.

Other hospice volunteers can provide similar insight and pleasure. Pet therapists are always welcome visitors. So are music therapists. Often a patient who isn't responsive to voices will still respond to music. And a session with a music therapist who plays your favorite tunes is fun for the caregivers as well.

Music therapy can even extend lives. One of the most amazing music therapy stories I ever heard was told to me by my colleague Terry Blaine. She was asked to visit a patient who, she was told, was dying of congestive heart failure. He had gone into hospice care soon after losing his wife of 57 years. Her music therapy intern went to see the patient and came back to Terry saying, "This man is dying of a broken heart." The intern visited the patient weekly and came to have a solid bond with him. Eventually, they put together some music the intern had written with a poem to his beloved wife the patient had written. When they first sang it together, the patient cried and cried. Over time, however, the song helped him come out of his heartbroken place and see that life still had good things in it, like grandchildren and the Yankees. The man left hospice and lived fully for another three years!

Spiritual Care Specialists

Hospice will also arrange for spiritual care counselors if you ask. Many of my patients never really had a relationship with a priest, pastor, rabbi, or other spiritual advisor. As they approach transition, they often feel the need for spiritual counseling even if they were never religious or spiritual at all in their earlier life. We can always arrange a visit for you. It doesn't have to be religious or involve prayer—we have both ordained and nondenominational volunteers. All are trained to focus only on the patient's spiritual needs. Their goal is to help you be at peace with yourself as the end approaches. I have seen how often spiritual care specialists can be very helpful for patients who have unresolved family issues, deep regrets about past actions, and other concerns about their impending death. Talking to a caring, sympathetic, nonjudgmental person who knows you only for who you are now can help dying people release emotions they would never want to express in front of their loved ones.

Unfortunately, spiritual distress doesn't always get resolved. I once had a patient who had served in Vietnam. He told me he had done a lot of bad things in that war and was very afraid to die because he thought he would go to hell for his actions. It was clear to me that he still had a lot of anger both about the war and his part in it. Beyond what he first told me, he didn't want to talk about it with me, a spiritual care specialist, or anyone else. He hung on much longer than I thought he would, and died with his fear and anger still there. I was very saddened by such an unhappy passing, because I know a spiritual care specialist could have helped him.

Practical Caregiving: Hospital Beds

Hospice patients often say they want to die in their own beds, but in fact, the best way to care for someone with a life-limiting illness is with a hospital bed. Unfortunately, a hospital bed doesn't always fit comfortably in the patient's bedroom. Also, we want to keep the patient on the main floor of the home so that the patient and the caregivers don't have to manage stairs. This means the hospital bed often ends up in the living room or some other downstairs room.

This can be very upsetting, especially for partners who have shared a bed for so many years. Still, a hospital bed is the best solution to both patient comfort and also a lot of caregiving issues. For example, the caregiver needs to be able to reach the patient from either side of the bed, which can't be done in a double bed, much less a king-size one. The head and foot of the hospital bed can be raised or lowered, which makes it easier for the patient to get in and out. Also, if the patient is having trouble breathing, raising the head of the bed helps quite a bit. Hospital beds also have side rails, which are extremely important for preventing dangerous falls from the bed. The rails help keep agitated, anxious, confused, or very restless patients from getting out of the bed and then falling down and hurting themselves because they don't have the strength to stand.

Spouses often want to stay in the room with the patient at night. They may end up sleeping on a lumpy couch or even an air mattress on the floor. I understand how important this final togetherness is, but we also have to make sure the caregiving spouse isn't getting worn out from lack of restful sleep. Until near the end, most hospice patients can be left alone at night. In fact, a patient may feel guilty about the spouse sleeping on an uncomfortable sofa bed. Many ask me to convince the spouse to get a comfortable night's sleep in his or her own bed, even if it is alone.

Practical Caregiving: Positioning the Patient in the Bed

Patient comfort becomes very important when someone is in bed most or all of the time. At this point, the patient is frail and is probably having skin problems. He or she is now very vulnerable to bed sores and skin injuries—a bed sore can develop in just ten hours. One of the best ways to keep the patient comfortable is very simple: Make sure the sheets are flat and smooth. Bunched-up sheets create areas of pressure than can injure fragile skin. To smooth the sheets while the patient is in the bed, smooth out and tighten the sheet on one side, then carefully roll the patient onto the smoothed sheet and do the other side. Keep the top sheet smooth but loose so it doesn't press down on the feet.

If you stop to think about it, when you're home in bed with the flu, you reposition yourself all the time. As your loved one becomes weaker, however, he or she won't be able to do that—you'll need to help. I ask the caregivers to reposition or turn the patient every couple of hours to help prevent skin breakdown and to keep him or her comfortable in general. Do this even if the patient is sleeping—you probably won't wake him. You don't need to do it at night, however.

For some reason, even very weak patients tend to slide down toward the foot of the bed and need help getting back up. The best, most comfortable, and safest way to move a patient in bed is with a draw sheet. I spend a lot of time with caregivers making sure they understand how to use one.

A draw sheet is regular flat bed sheet that's folded over in half and placed crosswise on top of the hospital bed sheet. When the patient is in the bed, the draw sheet should be under the area between the thighs and the shoulders, with the folded edge under the upper back. Don't tuck the ends in—let them hang over the side of the bed.

To move the patient, DO NOT drag him by pushing or pulling him up in the bed or from side to side. You're likely to injure the skin. Instead, use the bed controls to make the bed flat and raise it up to waist height so you're not bending over. Put down the bed rails if they were up. Roll the side of the draw sheet up until it's nearly touching the patient's side. Then, using your legs, pull steadily on the rolled-up part to move the patient upward in the bed. You can also use the draw sheet to gently roll the patient onto one side, which is very helpful when it comes to changing padding and making up the bed.

Using a draw sheet is much easier with two people, one on each side of the bed, but it can be done by one person pulling from one side and then the other. As your hospice nurse, this is one of the most important things I can teach you. I'll show you how and then we'll practice a few times to make sure you feel comfortable with using the draw sheet. I also recommend searching around on YouTube for training videos! There are a lot of these. They're meant for teaching bedside techniques to nursing students and aides, but they're very helpful for family caregivers as well. The videos cover a lot of useful topics and are short and easy to follow.

Practical Caregiving: Incontinence

As patients approach the end of life, they often lose control of their bladders and bowels. This is really upsetting to patients. It's humiliating and embarrassing for them, especially if they have to use adult diapers. In fact, the word diaper is so upsetting that we often say padding or incontinent briefs instead.

We have a lot of good ways to help with incontinence. We can put a portable commode by the bedside, which is easier for the patient than trying to get to the bathroom. If a male patient can't get out of bed, a urinal can be used. We don't usually recommend using a bedpan, however. They're tricky to use safely and comfortably with frail patients. It's safer and actually more comfortable for the patient to use adult diapers.

Once a patient accepts the diaper idea, he or she usually finds that they're unobtrusive and pretty comfortable. This is often a good solution. We can also use disposable pads, better known as Chux after the brand name, under the patient.

Keeping the area clean and dry is crucial for patient comfort and to avoid skin breakdown. Use warm water and mild soap, and pat the area dry gently with a soft towel. Don't rub! You may need to apply a moisture barrier cream containing zinc oxide and petroleum jelly to help prevent skin irritation. There are a lot of brands; choose a hypoallergenic, fragrance-free product.

The most important thing about dealing with incontinence is to maintain the patient's privacy and dignity. Make sure the patient is comfortable with any caregiver who is providing such intimate care. Tell others in the room that some privacy is needed.

In some cases, a patient near the end may not be able to urinate, which gets uncomfortable fast. In those cases, I'll insert an indwelling urinary catheter, also known as a Foley catheter, to drain urine from the bladder. The insertion is quick and not really painful, and once the catheter is in place it's not uncomfortable or painful. The catheter doesn't require much care—I can teach you what to do in just a few minutes. Because the patient is near death, not much urine is being produced, and the catheter will usually be in place for a few days at most.

Constipation from pain drugs is the more common bowel problem. It can be very uncomfortable. To prevent it, we put the patient on stool softeners and laxatives at the same time we start the pain meds. When the drug dose goes up, we have to increase the other doses as well. Because it's so embarrassing to talk about your bowel movements, sometimes patients suffer in silence from constipation rather than tell anyone about it. If your loved one seems anxious, uncomfortable, is gassy, bloated, or nauseous, constipation could be the cause. It can even be the cause of breathing problems. Increasing stool softeners and laxatives can be very helpful. Sometimes an enema is needed. Before you make any drug changes or give an enema, call your hospice nurse!

The only thing that's more distressing to my patients than urinary incontinence is bowel incontinence. Sometimes it's from the disease; other times, it's loose stools or diarrhea as a side effect of medications. Either way, when patients lose control here, they feel really ashamed and embarrassed. It's especially important to be reassuring and protect the patient's privacy when dealing with bowel incontinence. Some patients get so upset about bowel incontinence that they don't want to eat or drink or take the laxatives and stool softeners they need to counter the constipating effect of pain drugs.

To clean up, use toilet paper to wipe away the poop, then use an unscented baby wipe to finish. Use adult diapers and padding to help keep the patient clean and dry.

Practical Caregiving: Patient Clothing

Patients who aren't bedridden often like to get dressed each day in whatever clothing is comfortable for them. As the patient gets frailer and spends more time in bed, getting dressed is less of a priority. Instead, we focus on keeping the patient warm and comfortable and avoiding skin problems. A lot of patients hate wearing a hospital gown. Of course they do. The designs are boring and your butt hangs out, plus they're not that warm. Dying patients generally lose a lot of weight and don't have much body fat left, so they feel cold all the time.

One good solution is a large cotton t-shirt cut up the back. The cotton is soft, cutting it means the back can be pushed out of the way when the patient is lying down, and there's a lot of variety in designs out there. A shirt larger than the patient's usual size will help maintain dignity by covering the genital area when the patient is lying or sitting. You can use Velcro to hold the shirt closed at the neck. Fleece or flannel shirts and sweat jackets are soft and comfy. Warm socks help cold feet, but be careful here to avoid bedsores on the heels. Try cutting the heels out of the socks or scrunching them down.

Practical Caregiving: Daily Assessment

I ask caregivers to check the patient every day for his or her ability to walk and move around and for his or her ability to swallow. Why check the ability to walk, or ambulate, as we nurses say? Because above all things, we want to avoid a fall that could break a bone, cause a concussion, or create additional problems that could hasten the end. Why check the ability to swallow? Because the next thing we most want to avoid after a fall is choking or aspirating (breathing food or drink into the lungs). Even if the patient's abilities decline gradually, one day they will reach a point where walking has to be limited and we have to be very careful about swallowing. (I'll talk more about swallowing problems later in this chapter.) If you notice a sudden change in the ability to walk or swallow, call me at once. Otherwise, we'll talk about the changes when I make my regular visits.

Practical Caregiving: Avoiding Falls

When I visit a family entering hospice care, one of the first things I do is a home safety assessment. Top of the list is trip hazards. The last thing I want is for my patient—or any caregivers—to trip on a throw rug or lamp cord and have a bad fall. I work with the caregivers to get these problems fixed. Medications can be another trip and fall hazard. Some drugs can make the patient lightheaded, dizzy, or drowsy. Although we try to manage the meds so this doesn't happen, it's still a concern.

Avoiding trips and falls is really a matter of common sense. For example, clean up all spills immediately so nobody slips on a wet floor. Keep electrical and phone cords out of the way. Put away the throw rugs. If you want to cover that part of the floor, use a nonskid mat instead. Keep pets as much out of the way as possible.

I often have to help the family declutter the house, both to make room for the hospital bed and to avoid falls. We rearrange the furniture to make wide paths and remove trip hazards such as boxes, piles of papers, and so forth from walkways and stairs. Good lighting is also important for preventing falls, so we move the lamps around and add nightlights where needed.

We also make sure the stairs have handrails. I always suggest grab rails in the bathtub and shower and by the toilet. If that's not possible because of the expense or because of the home design, a sturdy kitchen chair can help with getting in and out of the bath seat in the tub. Instead of using the toilet, patients can use a portable commode, which has side rails.

A raised toilet seat makes it easier and safer for the patient to use the bathroom. A shower seat lets the patient bathe much more safely. Your hospice nurse can usually arrange to get these from a hospital supply company or pharmacy.

What's the single most important step you can take to avoid trips, slips, and falls? I thought you'd never ask. Wear shoes that fit well and have slip-resistant soles. Don't wear floppy slippers or mules. For patients who aren't up to much walking, I recommend socks with slip-resistant soles. They keep the feet warm and help avoid falls.

The greatest risk of falls comes when you're moving the patient from bed to chair or commode and back again. Again, this is where the hospital bed is so valuable. To get a patient out of bed safely, use the controls to help him sit up. Then use the controls to lower the bed as far down as possible.

Next, have the patient move to a sitting position on the side of the bed, with legs touching the floor if possible. Wait a bit at this point to let the patient's blood pressure normalize. Make sure the patient is OK and not feeling dizzy or disoriented. Next, hold the patient's arm above the elbow and help him stand up. Don't let go! Wait a bit to make sure the patient is standing on his own and isn't dizzy. Then, carefully pivot the patient onto the commode or into the bedside chair. Reverse the process to get the patient back into bed. Do things slowly and make sure to pause after each change of position.

Practical Caregiving: Skin Care

A big concern for hospice patients is skin care. Because they are frail, aren't eating much, and spend so much time in bed, hospice patients can easily develop pressure ulcers, better known as bedsores. Ulcers develop most often on the buttocks and heels, but patients can get them anywhere. The last thing we want for a dying patient is painful, oozing bedsores.

The best approach to bedsores is avoiding them to begin with. Your hospital bed will come with a special gel-filled mattress that helps keep pressure points that can break down the skin from developing. Pressure points are also why it's so important to keep the bedding smooth and avoid lumps and twists that can affect the skin. They're also why it's so important to move the patient every two hours, so that no body part is a pressure point for too long. To avoid bedsores on the heels, put a pillow under the ankles so the heels are hanging off and not touching the bed sheet.

If you think the patient is starting to get a bedsore, call your hospice nurse immediately. We want to treat the area quickly, before the situation gets worse. Every time you move or turn the patient, check the skin. Look for any area of the skin that is red or irritated or seems swollen or blistered—a nasty bedsore can develop in that area in just ten hours.

Another big skin problem for hospice patients is itchiness. This can be helped by using a moisturizing hand cream. Pick one that's hypoallergenic and fragrance-free. Itchy rashes may need a prescription cream.

Practical Caregiving: Shortness of Breath and Coughing

If there's one thing I hate to see in a hospice patient, it's shortness of breath, or dyspnea. We also call this air hunger, and it's painful to watch and even more painful to experience. I want you to call your hospice nurse immediately if any shortness of breath starts, even if it seems mild. Often we can talk you through ways to help.

If the patient is on oxygen, there might be a problem with the equipment, such as a kink in the tubing. Sometimes I find that the oxygen generator machine is turned off or unplugged! Other causes of shortness of breath include fluid overload, anxiety, untreated pain, and even constipation.

We can usually treat shortness of breath by dealing with the underlying problem. Any shortness of breath for any reason makes people feel anxious, which makes the shortness of breath even worse, so I always help patients with relaxation techniques. The healing touch of reiki is also very relaxing for people with shortness of breath. So does staying calm around the patient. If you're anxious, it's catching and will only make the patient even more anxious and short of breath.

Raising the head of the bed can help a lot. If the patient isn't already on oxygen, sometimes shortness of breath tells us it's time to start. Unfortunately, oxygen doesn't always help, but since it is painless and easy, it's generally worth trying. Most importantly, we use morphine, which is almost miraculous in the way it helps people breathe more easily. Some people worry that this will hasten the patient's death. Not so. The patient is dying; giving the morphine only makes him or her more comfortable as the end nears.

Coughing can be a real problem for some patients. We treat the cough depending on what's causing it. We can use various kinds of cough syrups and bronchodilators to suppress the cough. When the cough is bad and other treatments aren't helping much, morphine or other opioids can be very helpful.

Practical Caregiving: Loss of Appetite, Nausea, Vomiting

Hospice patients often lose their appetites as they get sicker. That's a normal part of their disease progression. Caregivers have to just accept that their loved one will eat and drink less, and will lose weight, as time goes by. Preparing favorite foods and special dishes may help tempt the patient's appetite a bit, but even that may not help. In fact, it may upset the patient to think that you went to all the trouble of making the favorite food and she couldn't eat it. Stick to foods you know the patient likes and can eat easily, and let her decide how much and when to eat.

If a patient is having a lot of nausea or vomiting, the first thing I have to do is figure out why. For example, constipation, a very common side effect of painkillers, can cause nausea. Once we know what the cause is, we can take steps to deal with it, such as antinausea medication. Nausea can rival pain as a cause of patient distress, so we take it very seriously and work hard to find ways to relieve it.

Caregivers can also help relieve nausea. Changing the patient's food can do a lot. Stick to bland foods such as mashed potatoes, yogurt, dry toast, plain crackers, and similar foods the patient likes. Small portions every couple of hours are better than larger meals less often. Avoid anything fried, fatty, very sweet, spicy, or with a strong smell. Keeping the room cool, with good air circulation to carry away any odors, also helps. So does keeping the patient's head elevated.

When a dying patient is having trouble keeping food down, the family often asks me about putting in a feeding tube. This is almost always not a good idea—as I'll discuss in chapter 6, the feeding tube will cause pain and discomfort and may even shorten the patient's remaining time. In fact, a feeding tube may go directly against the wishes your loved one has already stated in an advance directive. Likewise, surgery near the end of life to relieve a bowel obstruction will cause pain and distress for the patient. It may even shorten whatever time is left and could well mean your loved one will die in a hospital instead of at home. It's hard to see someone suffer, but you have to think about the patient's best interests and wishes first.

Practical Caregiving: Avoid Choking
A patient who can't swallow well or who has pain with swallowing is at serious risk of choking and of aspirating food or drink. Aspirating

means accidentally inhaling a bit of food or liquid into the lungs. This is dangerous, because it can cause pneumonia. Also, not being able to swallow well leads to poor nutrition and may even leave the patient feeling hungry.

There are a lot of possible reasons for swallowing problems. No matter what the reason, it's important to avoid choking and aspiration by being very careful with food and drink. Have the patient sit up straight when eating or drinking—this helps the food or drink go down the right way. Avoid crunchy or crumbly foods. Instead, stick to soft, easy-to-chew foods. Some good choices are yogurt, cottage cheese, thick soups, milkshakes, puddings, and anything pureed. Liquid supplements like Boost or Ensure are good. Thickening agents can be added to liquids to make them easier to swallow. Drinking through a bendy straw is often easier than trying to drink from a cup or mug. The patient should eat slowly and carefully.

When swallowing problems start, the patient will have trouble swallowing pills, too. Fortunately, we have a lot of other ways to give pain medication, including skin patches and sublingual tablets. The sublingual tablets go into the mouth, under the tongue or in the cheek. They're not swallowed. Instead, the tablet dissolves and the medication is absorbed into the bloodstream through the membranes of the mouth.. One reason I ask caregivers to assess swallowing each day is so that we can be prepared for the time when we need to substitute another delivery method for pain pills. The last thing we want is a delay in giving pain meds.

Practical Caregiving: Oral Care

Hospice patients may have oral problems such as mouth sores or dry mouth. Some may develop a fungal condition called thrush. Mouth problems are often caused by drugs, chemotherapy, or radiation therapy. We can treat thrush with an antifungal drug. For dry mouth, frequent small sips of cool water or ice chips can help. We also suggest using oral swabs to clean the teeth without brushing them and also as an alternative to sipping water for dry mouth. Toothettes, as they're called, are sold in pharmacies and medical supply companies.

Practical Caregiving: Personal Hygiene

Bathing, washing the hair, and shaving are all big morale boosters for patients. If the tub is no longer an option, I'll teach you how to give the patient a sponge bath in a chair or in bed. Dry shampoos work well when hair washing is needed. If pain is a problem, give the patient his usual pain meds half an hour before you begin a sponge bath. Your hospice nurse can arrange for volunteers to come by for hair styling and manicures.

Practical Caregiving: Stuff to Have

Hospice will provide you with a lot of medical supplies, including disposable diapers and pads (Chux), skin cream, Toothettes, and disposable gloves. What hospice doesn't provide are all the little things that make the patient more comfortable and help with her care. Here's some stuff you should have around the house: lip balm, baby wipes, draw sheets, adult bibs, and bendy straws. A notebook to keep track of symptoms and drugs, especially pain meds, is really helpful. A baby monitor/intercom is also great.

Should You Call 911?

If you're caring for someone with a life-limiting illness who is in hospice, you have to face reality. Your loved one has expressed a powerful wish to die naturally, without lots of painful intervention and futile medical care. That almost always means that you should not call 911, even if your loved one appears to be having some sort of crisis. Here's why: In most states, the emergency medical technicians who respond to a 911 call must, by law, treat the patient aggressively. That means, among other things, that they may have to do CPR if the patient isn't breathing or doesn't have a heartbeat. It's important to remember that if it's the law in your state, they must do this even if you have a Do Not Resuscitate order. So, a call to 911 could mean your loved one ends up on the receiving end of emergency care that's sterile, invasive, and unfriendly and leads to him being in the hospital on a ventilator. This is exactly what you went into hospice care to avoid!

How do you decide if the situation is an emergency? First, think about where the patient is along the course of his or her life-limiting disease. If the transition is approaching, emergency care will probably be painful and distressing and not in keeping with the patient's wishes for end-of-life care. Then ask yourself if the emergency treatment will result in any improvement in the patient's quality of life. In my experience, this doesn't happen very often. Also ask yourself if the patient would want aggressive care or palliative care at this stage. Many patients have said to me, "I never want to go the hospital again." And just to say it one more time, before you call 911, call your hospice nurse. We can almost always help you work through the issue and make the right choice.

And here's another good reason not to call 911: A few years back I had a hospice patient in her early 40s who died of breast cancer. Unfortunately, she didn't have a DNR order. Near the end, the family panicked and called 911. The EMTs came and, because there was no DNR order, had to do CPR even though the family asked them not to. After that, they started asking questions about drug overdose that made the family feel as if they were murder suspects. They were just doing their job, of course.

Pacemakers and Defibrillators

Many hospice patients have pacemakers that help their heart beat regularly. Some, especially those with heart failure, have implanted cardioverter defibrillators (ICDs) that give them a strong jolt of electricity if their heart starts to defibrillate, or beat in an uncoordinated way. You know those defibrillator devices they're always using on medical TV shows, where the doctor goes "Clear!" and then applies the paddles to the patient's chest? That's what an ICD is in miniature. And just as the patient on TV jerks when the electricity from the paddle hits his body, the ICD can be painful when it goes off. My patients tell me it's like being kicked in the chest. The jolt is powerful enough to knock someone over.

When a patient with a pacemaker is dying, there's generally no issue. The pacemaker is painless, it doesn't prolong life, and it stops pacing when the heart stops. ICDs are another story. They continue to jolt a failing heart back into action even when the patient is actively dying. That's painful, and it can prolong life by keeping the heart beating long after the patient would normally have passed away.

When we admit someone to hospice, we always ask about pacemakers and defibrillators. Generally we don't need to do anything about the pacemaker, but we do need to discuss turning off the shocking function of the ICD. Here's what we need to think about:

1. If we leave the ICD on, it could cause pain for the patient near the end of life.

2. But if we turn the ICD off, we're taking away one possible life-prolonging therapy. On the other hand, there's no guarantee that if we leave it on, it will help prolong life near the end.

3. Turning off the ICD doesn't cause or hasten death. It's not painful to turn it off.

4. Some devices have both a pacemaker and an ICD. It's possible to leave the pacemaker on and turn the ICD off.

Almost all patients choose to have their ICD turned off. This can be done at the cardiologist's office if the patient is ambulatory, or it can be done at home by someone from the cardiology office or the manufacturer. The process is very quick and painless.

Some patients choose to keep the ICD on. Others enter hospice so late that we don't have time to get it turned off. Hospice nurses carry magnets with them for these cases. We can use the magnet to disrupt the ICD and keep it from going off in dying patients. That's not the way we like to do things, of course, and we need the family's permission. Yet another reason to make advance plans that clearly state your wishes!

Chapter 6. Active Transitioning

We are so insulated from death in our society that many of the family members of my patients have never seen a dead person, except perhaps at a viewing in a funeral home. Very few have actually watched someone approach death, and even fewer have seen someone pass over.

What that means to me is that many of the people I work with have no idea what to expect or what to do as their loved one enters active dying and approaches death. That sometimes means they do things—or fail to do things—they regret later. Being prepared for the dying process means that family members and caregivers can help their loved ones pass peacefully.

What to Expect in the Final Days

As someone with a life-limiting illness approaches his or her final days and hours, he or she enters what we call the active part of the dying process. The changes of active dying usually follow a predictable path. In the bigger picture, the change begins when the patient is so weak that he or she can no longer get out bed. This usually signals that death is only days away—a few weeks at most.

The changes of active dying generally happen over just a few days or even less time. The changes can be hard for family members and loved ones to watch. It's important to remember that hospice care can do a lot to manage pain, breathing problems, and anxiety for the patient as the end approaches. We do everything we can to make the passing as peaceful and easy as possible. It's also important to remember that some symptoms that are upsetting to loved ones, such as eating and drinking very little or refusing food and drink, aren't painful to the dying person. At this time, we have to put away our own desires and focus on what is best for the dying person.

When you see the signs of active dying begin, call your hospice nurse at once. We can help you stay calm and manage the symptoms to keep the person comfortable.

Rallies

Sometimes, for reasons we don't really understand, a dying patient has a rally. The patient suddenly becomes more alert and aware, and may even sit up in bed and ask for a favorite food. One of my little old ladies rallied and asked for a cold beer! Another wanted pizza and Bailey's Irish Cream. There's no reason not to provide what the patient wants

A rally can last anywhere from a few hours to a couple of days. Most are short, but sometimes a rally can last long enough to create false hope of a miraculous recovery. Try to see a rally for what it is—a positive last moment. In my experience, death usually comes quickly after a rally, sometimes within hours. If your loved one rallies toward the end, make the most of it. It's probably the last chance you will both have for meaningful interaction.

Active Dying

When someone transitions to the active part of the dying process, it becomes even more important to provide care that focuses on comfort. Understanding what to expect makes it easier for caregivers to know the best ways to help the patient.

Sleeping, Confusion, and Restlessness

Someone who is actively dying slowly withdraws from this world. He or she usually sleeps a lot more, including sleeping a lot during the day. Caregivers should always allow the person to sleep. There's no reason at all to wake the person to give medication, food, or drink. Visitors should be asked to come back later. He may also withdraw psychologically, being less interested in and aware of what is going on around him and less interested in communicating with caregivers and visitors. As the dying person turns inward and becomes less responsive, loved ones sometimes feel hurt or ignored. That's not the case. What's happening is that the dying person is snipping the ties that hold him in this world. Understand that he is doing what he has to do.

Confusion is very common during active dying. The dying person may not know what day it is or what the time is, or even if it's day or night. He or she may not recognize familiar faces anymore, or may recognize you but not be able to remember your name or speak to you. Sometimes you might be confused with someone else, including people who passed away long ago. This can be upsetting for caregivers, who sometimes think the loved one no longer appreciates them or cares about them. Once again, we have to look at this from the dying person's perspective. He or she is now only partly in this world. It's not surprising that sometimes people who have gone before are now more real to him than the people he is leaving behind. Hallucinations, confusion, visions, and seeing people who aren't there are often comforting for the patient. In that case, don't try to bring him back to reality. Just accept that this is part of the process. Sometimes, however, the visions can be frightening or upsetting. I once had a patient who was seeing a big duck sitting on the end of his bed. This got him very agitated, to the point where he wouldn't let anyone go near that part of the bed. Needless to say, this made caring for him more difficult. When visions are bad, this can lead to severe agitation and harm to the patient—from falling out of bed, for instance. In that case, talk to your hospice nurse about anti-anxiety drugs.

If the dying person is confused, you can help keep him or her calm and aware by staying calm yourself. It's also helpful to have a calm, quiet environment around the patient. Massage and healing touch can be useful here. I've found that music therapy helps my patients quite a bit. We all know how listening to some favorite music can have a calming effect and help ground us. Even when the other senses aren't working well, hearing remains to the last. My patients are often responsive to songs from their younger years long after they have stopped responding to anything else.

As the end approaches, many dying people become restless. They may pluck at the blankets or do some other repetitive motion. They may move their feet constantly, almost as if they're walking. In a way, it's possible that they are "walking" toward their transition or to see loved ones who have gone before.

Restlessness can be a sign of a comfort problem, however. The patient could be having pain or could be uncomfortable from a blocked bladder or constipation, or for some other physical reason such as being cold. Breathing problems can cause restlessness. It could even be caused by an unresolved spiritual issue.

If the patient can no longer speak, restlessness may be the only way a caregiver can know there's a comfort issue. If the restlessness has a physical cause, then treating the problem—pain meds or inserting a catheter to empty the bladder, for instance—usually calms the patient. Many, though not all, dying people experience what's called terminal agitation and terminal restlessness. Even people who were always very calm and relaxed can become very restless or agitated as death approaches. This isn't caused by a comfort issue—it's just a normal part of active dying. Patients can become so agitated and restless that they're a danger to themselves. I've seen patients in this condition actually manage to slip through the side rails of a hospital bed and end up on the floor with a broken bone.

If the patient seems to be OK regarding pain and other possible causes of restlessness, anti-anxiety drugs or sedatives are strongly recommended to relieve terminal agitation and terminal restlessness and keep the patient comfortable and safe. As the end approaches, I try to make sure the caregivers have these drugs on hand and know how to give them. If you don't have the meds or if they don't seem to be helping, call your hospice nurse at once.

When we sedate a very agitated or upset patient, it's really no more than helping them sleep. At that point, they will probably sleep peacefully until death, which is almost always within a day or two. If we cut back on the sedation, the problems will return, but even worse because the patient's life-limiting condition has progressed.

Family members often ask me if sedation is the right thing to do.

They worry that it will bring death on sooner. That doesn't happen. The sedation is enough to keep the patient comfortably asleep, but not strong enough to hasten death.

Food and Fluids

Loss of appetite or inability to eat and drink is very common in the final weeks and days of life. Because offering food and sharing meals are so important to us as human beings, seeing a loved one unable to eat can be very distressing to caregivers.

Anorexia happens when a dying person loses her appetite or the ability to eat and drink. Cachexia is weight loss and wasting that happens when the patient doesn't take in enough nutrients. Loss of appetite and wasting are often final symptoms of the patient's life-limiting illness, especially when the diagnosis is cancer.

The loss of appetite could have other reasons, however. Pain can make people lose their appetites; so can the drugs we give for pain. Digestive issues such as constipation, nausea, or vomiting can reduce the appetite. Sometimes patients have mouth sores or other oral problems that make eating difficult. Severe fatigue can also make patients uninterested in eating.

We can help with pain and some of the other problems that could be causing loss of appetite, but loved ones need to remember that this is also just part of the dying process. The body gradually shuts down. In most cases, patients with appetite loss or wasting don't feel hungry or thirsty. They may ask for some ice chips or sips of cool water, but most don't want any food at all.

When dying patients in hospice start to eat less or not at all and begin to lose weight, family members often ask me about feeding tubes. If the patient has a living will or advance directive that specifies no feeding tubes or artificial feeding or hydration, I go over this with the family and explain that we have to follow the patient's wishes. When a patient comes into hospice only when very near death, unfortunately we often don't have an advance directive to guide us. That's when I have to explain why artificial feeding and hydration won't help with wasting or appetite loss. In fact, fluids or a feeding tube are much more likely to cause pain or even hasten death than to help with comfort care. That's because the patient's body is shutting down. Adding fluids or food can cause fluid overload, which in turn can make it hard for the patient to breathe and could even make it harder for her heart to beat. Instead of providing comfort, artificial feeding and hydration can cause discomfort and complications. That's not the goal of hospice care.

Food is such an emotional issue that families sometimes have a very hard time accepting the idea that artificial feeding isn't the right thing to do. They feel they have somehow let their loved one starve to death or die of dehydration. That's not true. The loved one has died of his or her life-limiting disease. The wasting and inability or lack of desire to eat were just the final symptoms. One of my patients stopped eating as he approached his end. His son was very upset by this and tried to spoon-feed his father. This was a big mistake—his father was barely conscious and ended up choking on the food and breathing some into his lungs. He then developed a bad cough from the aspirated food and ended up passing sooner and with more discomfort than if he hadn't been forced to swallow.

Instead of artificial feeding and hydration, dying patients can be offered liquids and their favorite foods every couple of hours or if they ask for them. All foods and drinks need to be given very carefully if the patient has trouble swallowing or isn't fully conscious. Usually the patient wants only small amounts, perhaps just a bite or two or a few sips.

At the end of life, the same sucking instinct that babies have seems to kick in. The patient may close his mouth tightly on a moistened swab, for instance. This could make you think that patient is very thirsty or hungry, but he's not. This is just a reflex action.

Breathing

People who are in the final stages of a life-limiting illness may have dyspnea—trouble breathing or shortness of breath. We often call this air hunger, because the patient is gasping for breath. As a hospice nurse I never, ever, want to see my patients be short of breath. It's very distressing and unpleasant for the patient. It's also very distressing to the family members.

When someone is actively dying, his or her breathing patterns change as death gets near. This isn't the same as dyspnea, and it doesn't need to be treated. Often the patient's regular breathing becomes irregular. The patient takes shallow breaths that are far apart. During Cheyne-Stokes breathing, as this is called, the patient may not breathe for anywhere from five seconds to a minute. This is when caregivers are most likely to panic and call 911. Please don't—as I explained in chapter 5 and will explain again below, this will only cause severe distress to the dying patient and to the family. This is a time when family members sometimes demand the patient be put on a respirator, or breathing machine. Again, this will only cause severe distress to the patient. It probably won't prolong life, but it definitely will make the time that remains traumatic and painful. The patient will almost certainly never get off the machine.

Sometimes patients will have noisy breathing—the death rattle. This happens because the dying person isn't swallowing very often, so saliva builds up in the back of the throat. It's not uncomfortable for the patient, but it's very upsetting to the family. Elevating the head of the bed can sometimes decrease the noise.

At the end, dying patients have apnea, or periods when they don't breathe at all, until eventually breathing stops entirely.

All the breathing changes that go with the final hours, especially the sound of the death rattle, can be very disturbing for family members. It's important to remember that the changes are normal as the body slowly transitions. When I explain what to expect to family members, I always remind them that the breathing changes aren't painful for the dying person. Hard as it is, they must just let them happen as part of a peaceful, natural death.

Other Changes to Expect

I've often found that patients who had a lot of pain earlier in their final illness have much less as they enter active dying. They need less pain medication than they were getting. On the other hand, sometimes a patient whose pain was well controlled suddenly has a lot more pain near the end. Because the patient's body is shutting down and doesn't respond to pain drugs as it once did, it can be hard to get the pain under control. As a nurse I don't like to see this happen, so I always encourage the caregivers to call me or the 24-hour phone to talk with a nurse or doctor about how to help the pain.

Someone who is actively dying doesn't usually eat or drink very much. That means that in the final period, the person doesn't produce much urine. What little there is usually appears darker in color than usual. The same goes for feces. Because the patient hasn't been eating much, he doesn't need to defecate much.

At this point, however, the dying person is usually incontinent, meaning he or she can't control urination and defecation. If the patient is retaining urine (usually because the bladder is blocked), I often suggest a urinary catheter at this point to help keep the patient comfortable. Putting the catheter in is quick and painless. Otherwise, to deal with urinary and bowel incontinence, we use padding or adult diapers. These help the caregivers keep the patient clean and comfortable.

Dying patients also have a strong grasp reflex. Just as babies will grab your finger and not let go, the patient will grasp anything placed in his hand. If you've been holding the hand of your unconscious loved one and try to pull it away, you may find that his grip actually gets stronger, as if he doesn't want to let you go. This can make it hard to leave the bedside, because you think the dying loved one is trying to hold you there. Important as loving touch is to the dying patient, this is a reflex, not something the patient is doing on purpose. It's OK to gently detach yourself.

Near the end, many patients find their vision gets blurry or dimmed. This can be distressing for the caregivers, but in my experience it rarely upsets the patient. It often helps to leave a soft light on in the room. Often patients will turn their head toward the light.

The patient may also lose the ability to speak. However, hearing seems to remain until the end. That means the dying person can still hear voices and other sounds even if he or she isn't responsive. To make the passing as peaceful as possible, try to keep the area quiet. Play music softly and speak softly. Remember that the patient can still hear what you say, so be sure you only say things you would want him to hear. Continue to talk directly to the patient, even if he or she can't respond.

As the body's circulation shuts down, the dying person's skin may appear bluish, pale, or mottled. It may feel cool to the touch. At this point the patient can still feel your loving touch. This is the time for final hand-holding and gentle caresses.

Keeping the Vigil

When a loved one is in the active dying phase, family members and caregivers often want to keep a vigil by the bedside. They don't want the patient to be left alone. The patient may have expressed a desire not to die alone. Also, our normal instinct is to want to be with the dying person to the end and not feel we have abandoned him or her. I know the dying person is grateful for the aura of love that surrounds him or her at this time. At the same time, keeping a vigil can be very stressful and exhausting for caregivers. It's OK for caregivers to leave the patient alone and take care of their own needs to eat and rest. If possible, try to arrange a schedule among the caregivers to take turns staying with the patient.

If the patient has a priest, pastor, rabbi, or other spiritual care advisor, he or she should be called when active dying begins. Many patients nearing their transition find a great deal of comfort from prayer and from traditional religious rituals.

Letting Go

Sometimes the dying patient seems to be holding on to life and not letting death come. Loved ones often see this as a positive thing. They'll say, with admiration, "Dad was a fighter to the end." Sometimes, however, dying people seem to be holding on until they get "permission" to leave. They may need to be reassured, for instance, that the loved ones they leave behind will be all right without them. When I see a patient who seems to be waiting for permission, I always encourage the family to say goodbye in a very positive way.

Even so, very often the dying person seems to wait for the caregiver to leave the room and then slips away. Many family members have told me, "I only left for five minutes to get a drink of water, and when I came back she was gone." Caregivers may feel very guilty about this, but in fact, I think the patient was waiting to be alone to spare the caregiver the experience of the final moments. If the final moments came when the patient was alone, remember that you were there for the whole time leading up to that point. When you look at the bigger picture, your care and love over the course of the final illness were much more important than being there for those last minutes. And in fact, the patient may have been glad you stepped away.

When I was a hospital nurse, I once had a patient who had had a massive stroke and couldn't speak. As he neared his end, his daughter kept a vigil over him. She was so exhausted that we finally persuaded her to go home and get some sleep. Soon after she left, her father went into cardiac arrest. Although he hadn't spoken a word for four months, he gripped the arm of the male nurse caring for him and said, "Tell my daughter I love her." He died just a moment later. I know he was waiting for his daughter to leave before he let go.

Patients sometimes hang on in order to accomplish something that's important to them. As a hospice nurse, I once worked with a woman who was 99 years old. She was very ill, but she really, really wanted to make it to 100. She hung on for 10 days, far longer than I thought she would, and died just a few hours after her birthday. I also had a patient who had been born in 1899 and wanted to live to see the year 2000 so she could say she had lived in three centuries. She did, living on well into 2000 before she passed.

Do Not Resuscitate

When active dying begins, it's normal for caregivers to feel panicky, to the point of wanting to call 911. Dying from a life-limiting illness is expected, however. It's not an emergency. Calling 911 isn't necessary. In fact, it could make matters much worse and cause the dying person a great deal of completely unnecessary pain and distress. In many localities, by law the emergency medical technicians must give CPR to someone whose heart has stopped, even if that person has written Do Not Resuscitate instructions. (Check back to chapter 5 for more on this.)

If you think active dying has begun and have questions or concerns, call your hospice nurse, not 911. We're there 24/7 to answer questions and give advice on end-of-life care.

Death

A dying person gradually begins to breathe more slowly (Cheyne-Stokes breathing), until finally the chest stops moving and breathing ends. The person no longer has a pulse. At the moment of death there may be a release of urine or feces. The person has finally transitioned when breathing and the heartbeat stay stopped, the eyes are fixed and no longer blink, and the body is completely motionless. The jaw looks relaxed and the mouth may be slightly open.

Sometimes muscle contractions a minute or two after the heart has stopped will cause the arms and legs to move; contractions in the voice box may make the body seem to cry out. This doesn't mean the person is still alive. Rigor mortis, or the muscle stiffening that normally occurs after death, usually begins about two to four hours after death. During rigor mortis, air may escape from the body, especially if it is moved. Again, this doesn't meant the person is still alive.

What to Do After the Death

After the patient has passed, there's no need to rush. It's OK to spend some time with the person to say goodbye, to pray, or to do whatever else is important to you and the family, personally and spiritually. If there are any religious rituals that should be observed at this point, take the time to do them in a meaningful way. Call the person's priest, pastor, rabbi, or other spiritual advisor.

When you feel ready, call your hospice nurse, no matter what time it is. Your regular nurse or the on-call night nurse will come as soon as possible—usually within half an hour—and start putting the final steps into motion. Your nurse will check the person for pulse and breathing, and will officially pronounce the patient dead. That time is the official time of death on the death certificate. My next job is to begin the death certificate paperwork with the primary care physician. This is usually just a phone call. Next, I'll call the funeral home and arrange for the body to be removed.

When I'm called to a deathbed, there's nothing more I can do to help my patient in life, but I can still help in death. I usually clean up any final body fluids and dress the patient in clean clothing, often with the loving help of a family member who wants to perform this last service. We also often tidy the room, removing medicine containers, commodes, and other signs of illness. This helps the family members have a positive last image of the patient.

Your nurse will also take away or destroy any prescription pain and anti-anxiety drugs that remain. Please don't take this the wrong way. It's not that we suspect you of wanting to sell the drugs on the street. In just about every state, it's the law—we have to do this.

Seeing the body being removed by the funeral home staff can be a very difficult time for the loved ones. The funeral home people are always very sympathetic and supportive, even when you call them in the middle of the night. They'll patiently wait until you are ready to let them remove the body, which they will do efficiently but very respectfully. Some family members want to watch the whole process, while others find it too hard. There's no right or wrong here. Your feelings at this point are your feelings. They're normal and nothing to feel guilty about. Even so, I strongly suggest that family members not watch this. In my experience, the finality of seeing the body leave the home is just too upsetting. I usually try to get everyone to gather together someplace else in the house and let me work with the funeral home people.

Your hospice nurse will also contact everyone who officially needs to be notified, such as the social worker and the hospital supply company. All that medical equipment, like the hospital bed, will be taken away very efficiently.

Hospice care doesn't end with the death of the patient. We're there to help you through the grieving process. Hospice nurses get to know their patients and their families well, and we grieve too when someone dies. It helps us continue to do our work when we know that family members are getting help and getting on with their lives after the death. I've seen how much bereavement services through hospice can help family members. Services such as individual counseling, family counseling, and bereavement support groups are free and can be very valuable. Please use them. (I'll explain more about bereavement services in chapter 7.)

Near-Death Awareness

Confused patients may be that way because of pain killers or other drugs or from dementia. People who work with dying patients, however, know that periods of confusion can often actually be what's called near-death awareness. The dying person may speak with or see loved ones who have gone before. My patients at this point also often talk about leaving, or having to go somewhere, saying things like, "I need to get ready for my trip" or "I have to cross the road." They may see very tall, beautiful human forms they describe as angels or guardians. They may also describe beautiful scenes of heaven. These visions give the dying person a sense of peace and joy and take away any fear of death.

Too often, caregivers mistake near-death awareness for anxiety, confusion, or delirium. They'll want to give the patient anti-anxiety drugs to "calm him down" or "bring him back to reality." If a caregiver has never seen near-death awareness, it can be disturbing. What the patient is experiencing isn't frightening at all. With one foot in this world and one foot in the next, he or she isn't anxious, hallucinating, or delirious—rather, the person is in a special state of awareness. Listen carefully to the patient if he or she describes the experience of near-death awareness. Don't minimize it as a hallucination or "just a dream." It's very real. Reverend Dave Wierzchowski, a spiritual care specialist at Family Hospice and Palliative Care in Pittsburgh, once told me about visiting a dying patient. As they talked, the patient kept glancing into a corner of the room. Dave asked him what he saw there. The patient replied, "I'm seeing my family in heaven waiting for me. I even see my mother-in-law, and she never liked me."

Someone with near-death awareness is on the verge of leaving this life. This is a time to pay careful attention, because what the person sees and says at this point can be very, very beautiful and even joyous. According to his sister, novelist Mona Simpson, here's what happened in Steve Jobs's last moments on earth: "Before embarking, he'd looked at his sister Patty, then for a long time at his children, then at his life's partner, Laurene, and then over their shoulders and past them. Steve's final words were: OH WOW. OH WOW. OH WOW."

Chapter 7. Caring for the Caregiver

Caring for a dying loved one can be a deeply rewarding experience. It can be the last act of devotion in a long and loving relationship. But as a caregiver, you might be so concerned with caring for the needs of your loved one that you don't care for yourself. Caring for someone with a life-limiting illness can be very exhausting, physically and emotionally. Often the primary caregiver for a dying patient is a spouse. When the patient and the spouse are both getting on in years, the spouse may not be in such great shape physically either. When the primary caregiver isn't a spouse, it's usually a child. Today, the child of an elderly parent is in what we call the Sandwich Generation. They're caught in the middle of caring for a dying parent or grandparent and also trying to manage their own families and careers. That's pretty challenging. It has big financial issues if someone has to take leave from work or quit, or ends up being let go because she (children who are primary caregivers are almost always daughters) misses so much work. That puts a lot of stress on family relations.

Caregivers may have medical issues of their own that mean they too need to get to the doctor, refill prescriptions, and take care of themselves. I see caregivers neglect their own physical health fairly often, and I see them neglect their mental health all the time. This isn't good. Caregiver stress can lead to physical and emotional distress—and that can affect how well you can take care of your loved one. I see caregivers struggle with feelings of anxiety, guilt, anger, resentment, and grief. They may feel unappreciated or taken for granted. They sometimes start to feel that life is meaningless and filled with too much suffering. All these feelings are normal. In fact, if you didn't have them sometimes, I would be worried about you.

Nobody can be upbeat and energetic all the time when caring for a dying person.

How Are You Doing?

Every once in a while, stop and ask yourself how you're doing. Are you feeling useful and needed? Are you getting enough support from other family members? Are you getting out of the house now and then? Do you feel trapped by the whole situation?

Think about your emotions. Are you feeling overwhelmed? Are you upset that your loved one is changed from his or her former self? Are you having crying spells? Do you feel edgy and irritable? Are you having trouble concentrating or making decisions? Do you feel lonely? Are money concerns keeping you up at night? Every one of these emotions is perfectly normal and even to be expected. Talking about them in a support group or with your hospice nurse, social worker, or spiritual advisor can be very helpful. Jut knowing that your emotions are normal can help you feel a lot better about them.

Also think about your physical health. Are you getting enough sleep? Do you have back pain? Are you eating properly? Are you taking your meds? Are you feeling ill in any way, like headaches or digestive problems?

Whenever I see a caregiver who's answering yes to a lot of these questions, I know the caregiver stress level is way high. That's when I suggest the caregiver see his/her own doctor for a checkup. I also strongly recommend getting some relief from the pressures of caregiving. I work with the social worker to try to get more home help aides for the patient. We also try to get other family members to pitch in more. Sometimes the main caregiver actually fights this, because as a loving spouse he or she sees the care as a sole responsibility. When we talk this through and I point out that harming yourself also harms the loved one, we can then usually come to an agreement about delegating some of the work. Friends, neighbors, and other family members can be asked to pitch in. Even family members who are far away can help by calling regularly, by contributing financially if needed and if possible, and by helping out with paperwork and any other tasks that can be done from a distance.

If there aren't any family members to help, I work with the social worker to use local resources, such as hospice volunteers, to give the caregiver some assistance. We also run support groups for caregivers, which can be very helpful for expressing your feelings in a safe environment and sharing tips for coping. Online support groups can also be very helpful.

Respite Care

Devoted as he or she may be—and I have seen many examples of amazing devotion—the main caregiver needs a break now and then. A few nights of sleeping through, instead of waking to take care of the patient, can work wonders for restoring the energy and spirits of a caregiver. Even a couple of hours off to go out to lunch with a friend can be a great morale-booster. I always urge family members to arrange time off for the primary caregiver. I tell them, "Do you want to go through this with your mother [or whichever family member] a year from now? Get her some help."

That's why I recommend respite care whenever I can. Respite means rest or relief, which is what many caregivers desperately need. Many hospice programs offer respite care, programs that provide temporary, short-term assistance with caring for someone with a life-limiting illness. The programs let the caregivers take some time away from the patient, even if it's just a few hours, to recharge physically and emotionally, knowing that the patient is in capable hands. Sometimes we can arrange for the loved one to spend some time in a residential hospice center so the caregivers have some time with less work and fewer pressures. Medicare and most insurance plans will cover the cost of five days of respite care in a residential setting once every couple of months.

Respite care can be important for the patient, too. Many feel guilty about being so helpless and putting their loved ones through so much trouble. I've had many patients bring up respite care for their caregiver. I once had an elderly male patient whose wife was a very devoted caregiver, spending all day with him and staying up most of the night as well. She kept saying to him, "How can you leave me?" Well, it wasn't as if he had a choice in the matter, but it made him feel that he couldn't let go in front of her. The family finally persuaded the wife to let his grandson stay by him one night so she could get some sleep. The patient, knowing he wouldn't be devastating his wife by dying in front of her, passed away peacefully that night. I have had a number of patients who passed very peacefully while they were in a residential hospice for respite care. I felt in each case as if the patient actually was waiting for the opportunity to leave so that the family wouldn't have to watch or from then on always associate the living room at home with death.

Hospital Care

Sometimes the care the dying person needs to be comfortable at the end becomes more than can be provided at home. This might mean a move to a residential hospice center, but more often it means hospitalization to deal with uncontrolled symptoms such as acute respiratory distress, intractable pain, a bowel obstruction, or uncontrollable vomiting. Hospitalization might also be needed for a sudden complication, such as a broken bone.

If you think your loved one might need to go to the hospital, DON'T PANIC. Call your hospice nurse! Don't call the ambulance or head to the emergency room until you've spoken to her. Often we can offer advice over the phone or stop by to help get the symptoms under control. Sometimes all that's needed is a change in pain medication or even relief from constipation. I have sometimes gone for more than a year, helping dozens of patients, without ever having to hospitalize any of them. I can almost always help you cope with the problem and keep the patient comfortable.

Hospitalization doesn't mean you stop being a hospice patient. In fact, you might be treated in the hospice section of the hospital, if they have one. Your hospice team will continue to manage your care while you're in the hospital. We make sure the hospital staff treat you for the problem in the least aggressive way possible and concentrate on keeping you comfortable. We also make sure they know your wishes about DNR orders and palliative care. Sometimes patients decide in the hospital that they want more aggressive care after all. That's perfectly OK. Hospice will continue to care for you when you come home, if that's what you want.

A big problem with hospitalization is that the staff is probably unfamiliar with your case. I find this means my hospitalized patients often don't get enough pain medication, especially at first. The other major problem with any hospitalization of someone with a life-limiting illness is that they're likely to get worse and die there instead of at home, as they want. Our goal with hospice care is to manage symptoms at home and avoid the stress of emergency room visits and hospitalizations. Even when a patient does need to be in the hospital, we work to keep the stay only as long as needed to stabilize the problem so the patient can return home quickly.

Grief and Bereavement

Caring for someone with a life-limiting illness means that you have to deal with grief and bereavement. Let's think a bit about what that means.

Bereavement is the word we use to mean the time that follows a death. There's no official length to the time period--everyone handles bereavement differently. Grief is the emotional response associated with the loss of a loved one. Mourning is the process of adapting to the loss. As with bereavement, mourning lasts as long as it lasts. Everyone comes to terms with the death of a loved one at their own speed.

There's a special form of grief that caregivers experience: anticipatory grief. You know, as you care for your loved one, that death is near. This leads to all sort of feelings, such as denial, mood swings, forgetfulness, feeling disorganized and confused, anger, depression, and feeling isolated and lonely. Add anticipatory grief to the physical stresses of caregiving and you can end up with health issues such as weight loss or gain and sleep problems. The caregivers I have worked with tell me that the worst part of anticipatory grief is the constant sense of anxiety they feel.

As a hospice nurse, my job is to help you cope with anticipatory grief. Many caregivers say to me, "If I feel this horrible now, how will I feel after my loved one dies?" I can't really answer that. What I can do is listen and help them find others to talk with about their feelings. All hospice providers run support groups and provide individual counseling for family members. If anticipatory grief is making you too upset or sick to be a good caregiver, think about getting help from hospice.

Bereavement Services

Hospice services don't end with the death of the patient. Hospice offers many bereavement services to family members, including grief counseling, special help for bereaved kids and teens, and support groups. If you don't want bereavement services after the death of your loved one, that's OK. But if you decide later on that you'd like some help dealing with your grief, all it takes is a phone call and your hospice provider will be happy to reinstate your bereavement services.

Grief is a natural response to the loss of a loved one. Everyone is affected differently. Some people cry a lot, while others feel numb. It's very common to have trouble concentrating and to have trouble sleeping. Some people may have strong feelings of guilt or self-blame. There's no right or wrong way to grieve. It's a process that can take a while, but eventually you'll return to your normal life. The bereavement services hospice offers can be very helpful for understanding your feelings, getting individual grief counseling, and getting support from others who are experiencing similar emotions. I know from following up with my hospice families that bereavement services really help. Some people have found good new friends through their bereavement group. In fact, I know one married couple who met in their spouse bereavement group.

Sometimes bereaved people experience what's called complicated grief. This is grief that is unusually severe or lasts longer than six months or so without getting any better. Complicated grief can interfere with your daily life and keep you from returning to your normal routine. For some people, complicated grief can turn into major depression. For others, it can trigger substance abuse. The possibility of complicated grief is another good reason to take advantage of hospice bereavement services. The programs are run by trained professionals who can spot complicated grief and help treat it before it becomes serious.

Family Conflict

When a loved one is dying in home hospice, the bulk of the care falls on family members. This can lead to a lot of conflict when the burden is uneven. In my experience, usually one or two family members do almost all the caretaking. Sometimes this is because of location—other family members may live too far away to help much. Sometimes other family members are nearby but have other responsibilities—kids, jobs, school, other family members who are ill—that mean they can't help much. And sometimes, for reasons of their own, family members just don't want to help. I've seen some families where the only thing they all have in common is some DNA—the conflict level between members can be very high.

When difficult decisions have to be made about the loved one's care, anger and old family resentments can get in the way, big time. Plus, these people have to make important decisions at a time that is incredibly stressful. And if the patient doesn't have any advance directives, the potential for disagreement about end-of-life care is huge. Even with advance directives, arguments can erupt right in front of the patient. People understandably aren't at their best when they're facing the death of a loved one.

It's not surprising that arguments can blow up over questions such as whether the patient should have an operation to relieve a bowel obstruction or antibiotics to treat aspiration pneumonia. When this happens, I always try to bring the focus back to the patient. We want to do what's best for his or her welfare. Sometimes this means I have to call a family meeting and make sure everyone knows exactly what's going on—family members sometimes conceal information from others. I also make sure everyone, not just the dominant family members or the loudest talkers, has a chance to participate. I can't fix what's wrong in the family relationships, so I stick to explaining what realistic expectations they should have about the patient's future. I try to explain why futile treatment, such as a respirator, doesn't meet the needs of the patient. Mostly, I try to get the family to focus on continuing to care for the patient at home in a way that ensures dignity and comfort. I tell the that the most loving thing they can do at this point is whatever is best for the patient. It's understandable that some family members would feel strongly that they should take all possible steps to prolong the life of their loved one. My job as hospice nurse is to help them understand that the quality of whatever life remains is what's important. If the patient has a living will or advance directives, we sometimes go over them so the family understands what their loved one wants. This can often relieve some of the unspoken guilt family members may feel over not being aggressive about treatment.

Visitors

When a loved one is dying, friends and relatives want to visit to pay respects and say goodbye. These visits can be very important to the dying person. They tell the person that his or her life had meaning and importance to others.

On the other hand, visits can be stressful and tiring, especially when the loved one is nearing the end. Ask visitors to keep their stay short, no more than 20 minutes max. Also ask visitors to call ahead and tell you when to expect them. If they want to come at an inconvenient time, say so. And if the loved one isn't up to seeing anyone, thank the visitors for their concern and say that now isn't a good time to visit. You could suggest sending a note or card instead.

Visitors to a dying person may feel very awkward and uncomfortable and not know what to say or do. Is it OK to touch the person? Can you use the words death and dying? What can you talk about? Should you bring flowers?

Flowers and other gifts aren't a good idea. If you want to bring something, bring a meal for the caretakers. Remember that the dying person may not look like his or her old self, but that person is still there. Try not to be shocked by appearances. Before you go in to see the dying person, ask the caregivers if touch is OK. If it is, avoid hearty bear hugs—hold the person's hand instead. If at all possible, see the patient alone so you can be open with each other. Conversation can be awkward, especially if the dying person can't really talk much or is confused or agitated. The patient is probably really tired of being asked how he's feeling and talking about his illness, so talk about something else—his favorite sports team, gossip from the office, news about family members, a story about your friendship with the person. If the patient wants to talk, especially to express his fears and concerns about dying, just sit quietly and listen sympathetically. If you have something to say to the person—an expression of love or appreciation, sharing a cherished memory—now's the time. You may not have another opportunity. And sometimes you'll sense that the right thing to do is just provide silent and loving companionship.

A visit to a dying person can be very emotional. The person might tell you how much you mean to him; you might want to tell the person how much he means to you. Expect tears.

Chapter 8. Life Is a School

When a person is dying, he or she has insight into what lies ahead for them and what the whole point of living means. If you are lucky enough and open to it, they will share this information with you. At this point in their life journey, their spiritual quadrants are so advanced that they have a direct tunnel of information from the higher realm. They have been visited by loved ones that have already passed. Their guides and angels, who have worked with them this entire time, have also visited. Things are very clear at this time. Many of my patients have communicated their glimpses of the higher realm as a gift for the living. I believe they hope to show us through their own example that death is nothing to be frightened of. When dying people are at this stage, a peaceful calm comes over them. Whatever fears of death and the afterlife they may have had disappear and serenity takes over. Without any judgment or blame, they will tell you that everything they have experienced here on earth was in order to learn to love unconditionally.

Life is a school with many tests and many teachers. In school, when you pass a test you graduate to the next level. In life, if you have learned what it is you came here to learn, then it is time to graduate to heaven! If we don't graduate and get the chance to move on to the unconditional love of the afterlife, that's OK. The God Source will let us go back to school again in a new life, with another chance to learn the lessons of love.

Do you ever wonder why sometimes a great individual is stricken with an illness or accident that takes his life early, while Mr. Grumpo, who drinks and smokes and is nasty to everyone, hangs on to a ripe old age? Well, Mr. Grumpo was not passing his tests, so he needs to stay here on earth until he's finally ready to graduate to the next and higher level. And although his early death seems unfair on the surface, Mr. Great Guy learned his life lessons well and taught many people what love is about. Now he himself is surrounded by the ultimate unconditional love of all. Mr. Grumpo is still a student who needs to learn more, which is why he's still here on earth, miserable day in and day out.

Open to the Afterlife

When people are at the end of their lives, their channels are wide open to the afterlife. I've been fortunate to be there when they have shared the direct feedback they're getting during this transitional time. Sometimes, dying patients will see a glimpse of where they are headed. Because as their hospice nurse I'm there to listen without judging, they will confide in me about what they have seen. Time and after time, these patients tell me the same thing: They were surrounded by the most incredible feeling of unconditional love. They were joined again with loved ones who had passed already. They felt pure peace. What they didn't feel was judgment, pain, or guilt. These people often tell me that they don't have the words to describe it, but that it was the most beautiful experience that they ever had.

If this is the case—and I have no reason to doubt them—then what is this whole life experience about?

There's an old saying, "You don't know what you have until you've lost it." I think dying patients appreciate this as they look back over their lives. Even so, the most significant meaning they take from their lives is the lesson of learning to love. Knowing that you are always loved by God, no matter what you do, is the most important lesson. You come from Pure Love and you will return to Pure Love. The life experiences you have are full of all types of lessons, all meant to help you learn to love.

Sounds simple, doesn't it? Well, let's take a closer look.

There Are No Accidents

There are no accidents. My studies in transpersonal counseling and my experience as a hospice nurse have convinced me that our whole lives are outlined for us before we come into them. As an unborn spirit, you do this in agreement with God and with your angels and guardians before you enter the body you're going to be in together. Before you're born, you actually take a look at what lies ahead for you, as if watching on a movie screen. You see in advance that at certain crossroads in your life to be, there are lessons, major or minor, to be learned. You'll have to make a choice, and that brings me to the biggest element at work here on Earth: free will. As a person, you have the ability to choose at all times. You can choose to do the right thing or the wrong, or the lesser of two evils. Sometimes your choice will be made for reasons of gaining power or the desire to hurt someone, but sometimes your choice will be for a higher reason, to experience the good of love. The choice to do something out of love is the ultimate lesson. We're in the school of life our entire lives only so we can learn unconditional love.

The single most important choice you make in life, however, is how you choose to spend your time. Life may sometimes seem to drag, but in the cosmic sense it is short and we have very little time here on Earth. Choose to spend your time wisely. Don't waste it!

Because our lives are mapped out ahead of time, there is an outline and an agreement that you make in advance. You know the parents you will be born to, the situation you will be born into, and you get a glimpse of the whole run of your life course. That's why there's no such thing as accidents. When you meet somebody by chance and that person becomes a good friend and a major part of your life, that's not an accident. Everything and everyone in your life is meant for a reason.

Even hurtful or negative experiences are all part of your life's larger plan. Every situation, even those that seem unfair or horrible at the time, is an opportunity for growth. You can get stuck in it or you can pass through it and come out enlightened. The choice is yours.

As you pass through your school of life, it's important to remember that while you want to learn the lessons you are being offered, it's OK if you don't catch on at first. Nobody is judging you, nobody is saying, "Oh, you really messed that one up." Not at all. With that in mind, we can learn to look at life situations in a different light. Do we want to be happy? Of course we do. Do we ultimately want to do things so that people love us? Yes! It's all about learning. The God Source doesn't judge you. If the God Source isn't judging you, why should you judge yourself? Learn from the experience—and learn not to judge as well.

Choosing How to Spend Your Time

When a person is at the end and is passing, they've gotten their spiritual eyes. What I've learned from them is that how you choose to spend your time in your life is the most important thing. At the end, nobody cares what you did for a living, what kind of car you drove, how much money you had in the bank. What matters is how you lived your life, no matter how outwardly successful or unsuccessful you may have been. Did you feel with your heart, did you go with your gut, did you follow your passion? Did you love people? Were you loved in return? Did you do your part on Earth as best you could? Those are the important choices. Did you make them correctly?

Angels and Guardians

The angels and guardians that work with you before you come into your body stay with you throughout your whole life. You may not realize they're there, but they are constantly trying to guide you and fend off bad things. They're your best buddies. When you sit quietly and let your mind talk to you and give you guidance, that's actually your guides and angels speaking. They're trying to give you information and guide you onto the right path. As I know from my dying patients, they will be there for you at the end of your life. At that point they will show up with more clarity and visualization. You'll see them and remember who they are. I've often seen dying children talk and play with their guides and angels. Kids haven't lost that spiritual connection. Adults will often say to these kids, "That's silly, there's nobody there," but the kids know better. As they approach death, they see their angels and guides in their totality. If you spend any time with dying kids, you realize that often the child is stronger than the adults and parents the parents.

Quadrants of Being

The body has four different presences within itself. They are four types of energy that relate to the four parts of your being: emotional, physical, intellectual, and spiritual. At different times of your life, different quadrants predominate and have a more profound effect on your thoughts and actions. Many people, especially when they're healthy and in the prime of life, are into an intellectual way of visualizing things. They want things that are tangible, that they can measure—they want proof.

But when even the most intellectual person is near the end of life, the spiritual quadrant dominates. When dying patients are faced with their mortality and they get in touch with their spiritual quadrant, it's almost like they have a direct link to heaven.

There is a strong energy around them that I find amazing. Here they are, facing probably the greatest fear that exists in our society—the fear of death—and yet they are surrounded by a sense of calm, peace, and tranquility.

As they prepare to leave life, they have learned the true meaning of unconditional love. They have gotten glimpses of an afterlife filled with love. I have seen many of my dying patients speak, in the hours before death, with beautiful, loving beings who can only be their angels and guardians. My patients seem to believe that these beings have been sent to them to help them leave this life and enter a different one.

I can't prove that there is life after death, but I also can't prove there isn't some continuation of consciousness. And what if there really is life after death, in some sort of heaven? How exciting that thought is! Wouldn't you change the way you are living now? Wouldn't you choose to spend your time in ways that would let you learn life's lesson of love?

Chapter 9. Learning to Love

The ultimate goal for all of us here on earth is to learn to love unconditionally. What does that mean? Unconditional means absolute, unqualified, completely, and without reservation or any holding back. Our lessons in the school of life are meant to teach us unconditional love of others, unconditional love of all things, and most of all, unconditional love of self. Of all these lessons, learning unconditional love of ourselves is the most difficult.

Cosmic Consciousness: Love of Everything
When a person is able to acquire unconditional love of self, a vibrational change happens within. It is at this time that he or she is able to connect with all things. This is called cosmic consciousness.

When you have unconditional love of self, you now connect to people and things on a whole new plane. When you go outside, you literally feel the energy of the trees, bushes, flowers, chipmunks, rocks—everything around you. All of it is connected to you!

The feeling is a wonderful harmony of togetherness. When you achieve this, you have the understanding and clarity that all things are part of a whole. There is no separation. Each and every one of us is connected. It is a beautiful realization that is achieved fully with self love. Think of it as a graduation present after learning all your major lessons. When you reach this level, your life's direction will most likely change, because your priorities have shifted. Enjoy this phase, because it took you a lot of work to arrive here.

I often see cosmic consciousness come to my patients when the end of their time on Earth is near. They're visited by loved ones who have already died. They're also visited by their guardians and angels, who tell them about what they are about to experience. At this point, my patients have amazing inner peace and aha! moments. This happens even when the patient made a lot of life choices that they regretted later on. Finally, it all makes sense to them. In this last stage of realization they experience unconditional love, without any judgment. They feel all is forgiven and all is love.

I've learned from my patients that the entire life experience is about learning to love. Every experience you have here on Earth is a chance for you to learn to love. You have the free will to decide that every experience, even a bad one, is an opportunity for love. Every experience, even the bad ones, happens for a reason. It might not always be clear at the time, but when you look back on something you can have your aha! moment. You can say, OK, now I get it, that's why that happened. Now that I'm down the road from it, I can see how that experience helped me evolve and become a more loving person.

What happens when you don't get it right away, don't look at all experiences as a chance to learn? The situations repeat until you do learn. The circumstances might be different, with different players, but the lesson to be learned is the same. Until you get it, until you master that particular lesson and graduate from it, you'll get it again. We all know people who continue to have the same challenge and continue to not learn from it. You might ask yourself, why don't they ever learn, but you also need to reserve judgment. After all, don't you face some challenge that keeps repeating?

Loving Others

Everything you do, say, or think has a ripple effect, just as when you toss a pebble into a pond. When you're young, your parents are the most loving beings you know. In fact, the way your parents love you while you are very young actually defines the way you develop for most of your life. We can all remember a time when our mother got angry with us and we were devastated, like it was the end of the world. That's how profound the love of your parents is. The meaning to life's journey is learning the same unconditional love we got as small children. If we don't experience that love as young children, the cycle of emotional development is badly disrupted. If you don't know from your earliest memories what unconditional love is, you will need to set off on a sometimes rocky path of lessons to learn it. The first lesson is that every one of us can attain unconditional love, starting with unconditional love of our selves.

It's a part of the life experience that we'll be hurt by others—that's just a fact. The question is, what do you do with that pain? Do you turn it inward? Do you turn it outward? Or do you look at it for what it is? Painful times are inevitable. We have to accept them as part of life's larger lessons.

Every difficult experience you have, every pain you go through, is an opportunity for growth. That's the ultimate point of living life. You're meant to experience something and process so you understand the clarity within it, not with anger or negativity but just by letting it be what it is and using it to get to a higher place of love.

Keep an open mind for all experiences. I'm not saying you should belittle tragedies or deny the pain you're feeling or the significance of how hurt you can be by a situation. What I'm saying is let it be there and then allow yourself to open your thoughts to the point where you can look at them from a bird's-eye view and see the bigger picture. Try to remove the emotion and look clearly at the lesson to be learned.

I want to make it clear that choosing any one of these options is acceptable and comes with no judgment. The ultimate goal is love. The third choice—accepting our experiences for what they are—would allow you to achieve that the quickest, but it is your free will to make the choice you want.

The Ripple Effect of Childhood Experiences

Our experiences in childhood have a long-lasting ripple effect on the rest of our life. They affect how we feel about ourselves, how we relate to our families, how we choose our friends and spouses, where our careers take us, how we treat our own children, how we choose to spend our time, and ultimately, how we die. The ripples of our own life intersect with the ripples from the lives of others.

Children who grow up in loving families usually grow up to be secure adults. Even in loving families, however, things can happen that will send ripples onward for the rest of a child's life. Love helps overcome the impacts of divorce, death, poverty, poor living conditions, bad schools, illness, and other bad situations, but nobody is completely unaffected by these experiences. The difference is that love makes even bad situations easier to manage. If you grow up getting and giving love, you will be much more able to learn life's lessons and spend your time wisely.

Sadly, many children grow up in circumstances that not only lack love but are abusive. Childhood abuse can come in many different forms: sexual, physical, emotional, or any combination. The pain can be so profound on children that they actually block it out in order to survive. Abused children can't love themselves—and that means they can't love others. They often are so damaged that the concept of unconditional love is forever closed to them.

The most common type of emotional childhood abuse is conditional love. As parents and individuals, everything seems to have an if. For our children, it's: I will love you *if* you get good grades, *if* you act the right was, *if* you do what I say. Very early on, children abused in this way learn to put all types of conditions on love.

When you're hurt or betrayed as a child, you're scared because you're small and vulnerable. You can't defend yourself against an adult, and the shock of the pain/betrayal leaves you paralyzed. This abuse manifests and has a profound effect on your adult self. Many, many times an abused child will feel that somehow it was his or her fault. They will carry that feeling with them for a very long time. The ripple effect of childhood abuse spreads out through entire families and entire lifetimes. It is very hard for abused children to learn to love others, and it is even harder for them to learn to love themselves.

In adulthood, abused children often follow a path of self-destruction through behaviors such as drug abuse, alcohol abuse, promiscuity, and inflicting pain on others as a form of power. A child suffers abuse that isn't his fault, then the adult child takes part in behaviors that abuse himself and others. The behavior simply confirms to that child/adult that he is a bad person, not deserving of love. It will be very hard to achieve a place of self-love unconditionally on this type of path.

Unconditional Love of Self: The Ultimate Journey

The hardest thing to achieve is to unconditionally love yourself. In order to do this, we must learn forgiveness. We need to forgive ourselves, and to do that we need to forgive others.

If we start from the beginning and look at life for the journey of learning that it is supposed to be, then we can forgive those who have caused us pain early on. In fact, they are key players in helping us reach unconditional love. They actually deserve our thanks, although we do not need to do that in person if it's not appropriate. This may seem contradictory. Why should we thank someone who abused us or caused us pain, especially when it was done deliberately? It's because there are no accidents in life. It may you take a long time to realize it, but you learned lessons from those experiences. The lessons are part of the who you are today. They're now an opportunity for further learning about love. Through forgiveness, you learn to love others, even those who harm you.

Once we acknowledge forgiveness to them, we must forgive ourselves for any negative behaviors and pain that we have caused others. By understanding the ripple effect of early experiences, you come to realize the source of your lack of love, negative behaviors, and poor choices. With this greater self-awareness comes self-forgiveness and greater self-love. Greater self-love also means greater love for others. This love gives you the inner resources and desire to repair any damage you have done to others. We can take this step knowing that we have never been judged by the God Source energy, and that any poor choices we have made only contributed to our own suffering. Without knowing it, we have had God's unconditional love the whole time.

It is the most challenging thing to forgive yourself. However, it is the *only* way to achieve the ultimate love you were meant to experience.

Chapter 10. Transition

I love the word transition, because that is the correct meaning of what death is. Death by definition is final, but the word only pertains to the physical body that was your "temporary housing" here on Earth. Transition is the changing of energy from one form to another. If we go back to science for a moment we know that thought is energy, energy is matter, and matter can only change form—not disappear.

On Earth, in our physical bodies, we are vibrating at a third-dimension frequency. You may not know it, but your vibrations are like the radio waves that are all around us. We don't see them and we don't feel them. We can only hear them with an antenna and when we're tuned to the right frequency.

It's the exact same way for our bodies. We live in a physical, three-dimensional world, but as we approach death, our energy vibrates at a higher frequency. Eventually it leaves the body it is in for good. This is only the end of your temporary housing. You as a healthy spirit continue to exist.

Being at the bedside of a dying patient is a privilege and an honor. It is imperative in my job to assist the patient and family in every aspect of the transition. Most importantly, my job is to make sure that no one should ever have to be in pain at the end of life. Good symptom management and care allow for a healthy departure. Good treatment at the end of life lets my patients focus on the life to come, without the distraction and distress of pain.

Getting Your Spiritual Eyes

As dying people get closer to transition they actually go back and forth to the higher realm. They are given glimpses of where they are going and they are reacquainted with loved ones and their angel guides who are waiting for them. As a hospice nurse who has seen transition many times, I can tell you this is an amazing experience to be part of. As transition nears, a person who has been restless or uncomfortable through the dying process becomes tranquil and serene. I have even seen some of my patients excited by the presence of departed loved ones that they have not seen in a long time, coupled with the confirmation of a heavenly afterlife.

I recently had a man at the end of life who said that his father, grandfather and uncle were in the corner of the room, waiting for him. His family shared with me that this trio had been to see him seven months earlier, when he was in the intensive care unit of a hospital, and told him it wasn't time yet. Now they were back. They helped this patient cross over for good.

As my patients go back and forth from this world to the next, they try to share their experiences. The unconditional love and all-knowing that they experience in their travels brings a peacefulness that is heartwarming. The pearls of wisdom that they will share are like those of a school-aged child. The spiritual light bulb goes on and everything is in perfect sync. At that point I often see a beautiful white haze around them, almost like a sheer gauze, and they look incredibly peaceful and content.

When a person leaves his physical body, he is in perfect physical form. There is no pain, no fear, and any physical ailment the body had is gone. At this time the person has a total awareness of all things all at once. There is no time or space as we know them. The person is accompanied by spirit guides, angels, passed loved one, and passed beloved pets. It is a completely loving environment. There is a transition —a sense of going on a trip, through a tunnel, across a bridge, across a meadow of beauty. On the other side, you are greeted by the most vibrant light of love, a love that words cannot describe. An unconditional, nonjudgmental, loving energy fills every part of your being and soul.

You are now within the God Source energy, and with *no judgment* you go through *your* life review. It is said to be like a flip book.

You see every choice you made, every word you spoke, every thought you had. You see how all these things touched others and had a ripple effect throughout your world.

You and God look at every choice you made. You see how your free will on Earth gave you—and you alone—the opportunity to choose the life you led. You see, without judgment, that there absolutely are circumstances that happed to us that seem unjust or unfair. It is how *you chose* to deal with them that made the difference. Did you choose to embrace growth from a painful experience, or did you choose to be angry, for example, and then act on that basis? When you review your life choices, you are looking at the school of your life. It was designed to teach you unconditional love. The lessons came in a variety of forms, packages and teachings. The hardest lesson to learn is loving yourself unconditionally. When you achieve that, you can love all things. If you have learned what you were sent here in life to learn, then it is time to graduate to heaven.

Near-Death Experiences

As a hospital nurse, I've seen a number of patients have near-death experiences. That's when a patient "dies" but is brought back to life by the doctors and nurses, usually through CPR or using electro-shock to make the heart beat again. Just about every patient who has experienced near death report similar sensations. They all say they had the sense of being above their bodies and looking down on themselves. They feel that everything they knew when they were inside their body remains. Who they are is still intact. At the same time, their physical body—their temporary housing here on Earth—is on the bed. These people have very clear memories of what happened to them during their resuscitation, even though from a medical point of view they were completely unconscious. They can tell you who came into the room first and repeat verbatim what everyone said. They also say that then they woke up and were back inside their body, just as they were before but now they have these amazing memories.

In every culture, people who have had near-death experiences report similar sensations. They pass over a bridge, through a tunnel, across a stream—they all experience some sort of transitional sense of going on a journey. They then enter the beautiful light of unconditional love surrounding them, a love with no judgment, no fear, no anxiety, no pain. They all say that this is the most loving experience they have ever had. It's so loving that they don't want to leave it and return to life on Earth. They're told, however, that it's not their time yet and they have to go back to be with their loved ones. Often these people experience the sense of meeting with God and having a life review. They describe it as sort of movie with your whole life passing very quickly before you in quick little pictures. While they watch, they feel nothing but love—there's no sense of judgment on how they lived their lives. You finally understand the ripple effect your actions had on others.

I believe these people have been given a glimpse of what heaven is and what their path will be when their time finally does come.

A Good Death

The dying teach us so much about living. That's the gift they give us at the end--that insight into their spiritual lives, what they've learned from living, and what they would change if they could do it again. At the end, they know what's really important about life.

To me, a good death means that the person has loved and lived life fully. He or she has done what they were sent here to do. They've made an impact—their life has made an impression on others.

Does this mean the person was always a good person? There's no such thing as a bad person, just people who sometimes don't make the right choices. Even someone who made a lot of bad choices in life can still, when dying, look back and say I have no regrets, I had a good life, I did what I needed to do, and now I can be at peace and have a good death.

What these people have taught me is to live your life to the fullest. Don't waste time. Do what you're here to do, love everyone and everything, and you can have a good death.

When you've learned unconditional love and have no regrets, you've passed life's hurdles and can move on. That's what considered a good death.

I've been at many bedsides for dying people in home hospice care. I'm always a little amazed at how hard it is for the family to accept that their loved one will be passing soon. They go into a state of shock; a lot of times, at least one family member really falls apart. They don't know what to do, they don't know how to handle the word death, they don't even know how to talk to the dying person. Our society's failure to admit the fact of death is a shame. At this critical time in a loved one's existence, families shouldn't become dysfunctional (or even more dysfunctional than they already are). Instead, they should be talking with their loved one, making sure he or she is comfortable and pain-free, and making sure the person feels loved and safe. Now is the time to share stories of your experiences together and what they meant to you. Most of the time, in my experience, this doesn't happen. In fact, often the patient seems to be the healthiest person in the room. That's when I often share a special moment with my patients. The family members are crying uncontrollably, but the patient is having clarity. He or she will share it with me because the family members aren't capable of listening. It is a remarkable opportunity to communicate with someone and gain insight into the next world.

Dying people can give you the greatest gift of all—they can teach you the true meaning of living.

Afterword: Hospice in Africa

In most of Africa today, the concepts of hospice care and palliative care are largely unknown. The need, however, is huge and urgent. In sub-Saharan Africa, HIV/AIDS continues to claim the lives of over three thousand people every day. Almost as many die of cancer each day. Providing care for the dying places a very heavy burden on women and children in the region. In Zimbabwe alone, where there are more than a million orphans, young children are caring for dying family members.

This tragic situation is slowly changing as hospice organizations build their skills and capacity. For example, Island Hospice in Harare, Zimbabwe (www.islandhospice.org), is working with the U.S.-based Africa Hospice Initiative (www.africahospiceinitiative.org) to fund hospice training and education and bring hospice care to a population that badly needs it.

Suzanne O'Brien is actively involved with the Africa Hospice Initiative. A portion of the proceeds of this book will go to fund AHI's initiatives.

Acknowledgements

Many people helped bring this book to life. I would first like to thank Susan Bang and Emily Collins of Bang + Collins Public Relations. Your skill and expertise in putting this product together was key.

Sheila Buff, I could not have done this without you. I will miss our coffee sessions and petting Daphne's ears. Thank you.

To my sister Lauren: Thank you for always being there, sis. I love you!

To the women who work at Vassar Brothers Medical Center on South Circle 5: You are the hardest-working group of women I have ever known. The patients are truly lucky to have a group like you. Thank you for letting me be part of your team.

To all the people at Hospice Inc. of Dutchess County and Ulster County: The work you do every day is so valuable and so appreciated.

To Terry Blaine, head of music therapy at Hospice Inc. in Dutchess County: Thank you for your inspirational stories. You are amazing.

To Greg Jena and his staff at Family Hospice and Palliative Care in Pittsburgh: Thank you for your help and for sharing your wonderfully inspiring stories.

To all hospice workers everywhere: Your love and dedication are priceless.

To all hospice families everywhere: Thank you for opening your hearts and homes and letting us work together at this very special time.

And lastly, to my son Nicholas: You reinforce the meaning of unconditional love every day!

About the Author

Suzanne O'Brien, RN, is an experienced hospice nurse, hospice advocate, and motivational speaker. Trained in both conventional medicine and spiritual and alternative healing, she brings a holistic approach to hospice care. Suzanne uses her medical training and natural gift of empathy to help her patients and families make the transition from life to death through the final months, weeks, or days, making sure their physical, emotional, and spiritual needs are being met. In *Life, Love, and Transition,* she shares the spiritual and practical lessons she has learned at the bedsides of dying patients. Her experience has taught her that our duty to the dying is to care for them holistically at the end of life. They must feel comfortable, pain-free, and dignified. Having an honest conversation about death, with the dying person and their family, is integral to her philosophy.

For more about Suzanne's work and her speaking schedule, see her website, http://lightenup444.com.

Made in the USA
Middletown, DE
03 October 2015